ROCKS OF AGES

Scribed by Ras Ben Anu Israel
Technical Support and Guidance provided by Ama Khem Anu Israel
Edited by Chanel and Mildred Cook

Copyright 2000 by B. Hopson

ISBN 0-9700646-9-1

Those Four Sounds™

Contact Those Four Sounds at:

E-mail Address: www.Thosefoursounds.com

Mailing Address:
Those Four Sounds
PO Box 25637
Philadelphia, PA 19144

ROCKS OF AGES
Ancient Technologies for the New Millennium

Scribed by Ras Ben

PART THREE:
Aya - Spiritual Technologies for the New Millennium

PART FOUR:
Asase Yu Duru -The Earth is Heavy

PHOTO & GRAPHIC CREDITS

Graphics by DB Design

Adinkra symbols on pages 8, 40, 92
Cover Art, The Rocks of Ages (front cover) and
The Inner Ark (back cover)
Model of Hydrogen Atom on page 11
The Spectrum of Creation on page 12
Map of the Ancient World on page 68
Kemetic Ark of the Covenant on page 73

Photograghs by DB Design

Vibes Alive Broadcast Station on page 182
Philadelphia Skyline on page 173
Pyramid chamber on page 192
Ancestral Alter on page 132

Typography by DB Design

Illustrations by Ras Teoderas (Carlos Williams)

Crystal Power on page 22
Melanin man on pages 28
Black Fist on pages 31
Mikael Slays the Beast on page 139

Photographs by Angela Muhammad

The Synergy on page 26
Thy Rod and Staff Series on page 186-187

Photograph by Patrick Ridley

Washington Monument on page 173

Photographs by Ras Ben

The Great Khuti on page 169
A Tekhen on page 169
Sacred Water on page 213
A Sacaphagus on page 50
Kemetic amulets on page 52

Chart by Gerald 'Assagai' Smith

African Relationships on page 131

Introduction

Rocks of Ages is an African-centered survey of stones, crystals, gems, and minerals as resources for a spiritual technology. 'Spiritual technology' means using tools (technology) for creating life force (spirit). It explores how traditional African cultures have used sacred stones historically, as well as principles for using sacred stones to enhance life force in the next millennium.

As an African-centered book, the perspective comes out of the African worldview, and People of Color are the target audience. However, great effort has been taken to be universal in respect and love to all peoples of the world. The goal of *Rocks of Ages* is harmony for humanity.

Rock of Ages addresses many spiritual issues, but is not religious or dogmatic. The information is empowering for people of all faiths, as well as atheists and agnostics. It is a practical guide to applying a spiritual technology - using tools for creating and enhancing life force.

Rock of Ages is grounded in the basics of physical, metaphysical, and medical sciences. However, a great deal of effort was taken to explain the information in a clear, understandable fashion. One need not be a gemologist or physicist to understand the text.

There is some creative use of the English language employed to make the meaning of some words relevant and culturally centered for Africans in the Americas.

I pray this book will provide empowering information.

Akoben

Akoben

Akoben is a **summons to collective action** and a **call to arms.** In the **Rocks of Ages**, *Akoben* calls to the reader's awareness that the African struggle for a free mind and Self-determination is a universal struggle. There is a spiritual dimension to the fight against oppression and injustice. The battle to establish truth, justice, righteousness, harmony, love, and divine order is occurring throughout the universe.

Akoben summons one to realize that **the weapons of power in a universal struggle are universal principles.** Laws that are true and consistent throughout creation are the most powerful weapons Africans can apply in the universal struggle waging on planet Earth.

Concerning the *Rocks of Ages,* an important universal principle is **Everything in Creation is Vibration.** Everything in the universe – from the highest frequency of radiation to the densest form of matter - is vibrating energy particles. Therefore, **the ultimate approach to gaining Self-determination of one's destiny and reality is to gain mastery of the vibrations in one's external environment and inner-world.**

Akoben says that **the most powerful tools Africans have for gaining mastery of their vibrations is melanin and sacred stones.**

AKOBEN!

Akoben -
The Melanin/Quartz Synergy

Everything Is Vibration

The use of crystals and sacred stones as tools for a spiritual technology is based on a key law of the universe: Everything in creation is vibration. It is a universal law that *everything,* from the highest frequency of radiation to the densest form of matter, is essentially vibrational energy. This universal law is a 'scientific fact' that has been verified by Western science.

Scientists know that matter is composed of molecules, and that molecules are composed of atoms. Atoms are composed of two primary particles: positively charged protons that form the atomic nucleus, and negatively charged electrons that spin rapidly around the nucleus. These particles bond together through an intermolecular force that is a form of electromagnetic attraction. Thus, in physics, atoms are considered to be vibrating energy particles (protons and electrons) that weave and intertwine with each other to form creation. Physics literally is defined as *the study of energy.*

Model of Atom

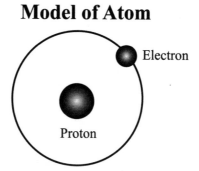

Matter is the densest form of energy. However, depending on the frequency of vibration, energy will manifest in one of three basic forms.

- Electromagnetic energy (The highest spectrum of energy)
- Sonic energy (The mid-range spectrum of energy)
- Matter (The lowest spectrum of energy)

Electromagnetic Energy:

This spectrum of energy contains the highest frequencies of energy in creation. Electromagnetic energy consists of radiant atomic particles (protons and electrons) that travel very fast. The average speed of these moving particles is around the speed of light. In physics, an atomic particle in motion is called a photon. Photons move through creation in wave-like patterns. The size of the wave determines the frequency of the photon's energy. The shorter the wavelength, the higher the frequency; the longer the wavelength, the lower the frequency. Even though photons move in wave-like patterns, the path that a photon travels is a straight line called a ray. Photon particles radiate, or stream out from an energy source in a straight line. For example, sunlight is radiant energy that radiates from the Sun. It is composed of various photon particles that stream forth from the Sun at the speed of light.

In the study of Physics, the electromagnetic spectrum is divided into eight sections. These divisions are based on the type of particle (i.e. - proton or electron) that composes the radiation; as well as the size of the radiation's wavelength. The eight sections of the electromagnetic spectrum are as follows (from the highest to lowest frequency) cosmic rays, gamma rays, x-rays, ultraviolet radiation, optical light, infra-red radiation, radio frequencies, power frequencies, magnetism:

ELECTRO - MAGNETIC SPECTRUM

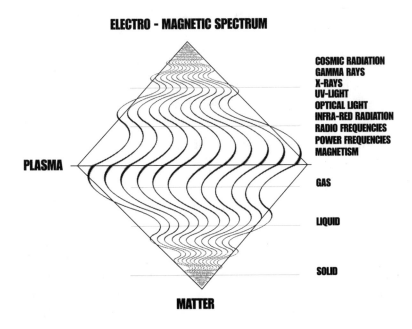

COSMIC RADIATION
GAMMA RAYS
X-RAYS
UV-LIGHT
OPTICAL LIGHT
INFRA-RED RADIATION
RADIO FREQUENCIES
POWER FREQUENCIES
MAGNETISM

PLASMA

GAS

LIQUID

SOLID

MATTER

Cosmic Rays: Also known as hard gamma rays, cosmic rays are extreme high-energy protons that have very short wavelengths (10^{25}-10^{22} hertz).[1] These particles are the highest frequency of energy in creation identified so far. They create super high-energy particle showers when they collide with Earth's atmosphere. The primary source of cosmic rays is the Black hole at the center of the galaxy, also known as the galactic core. Neighboring galaxies are also a source of cosmic rays.

Gamma Rays: Gamma rays are high-energy protons that have short wavelengths (10^{22}-10^{19} hertz). The primary sources of gamma rays are the Sun and neighboring stars; they are also released from terrestrial radioactive matter. Gamma rays are radioactive energy, meaning that gamma energy particles can penetrate and break down most forms of matter. Overexposure to gamma rays causes radiation sickness, in which the body breaks down and decomposes on the molecular level.

X-rays: X-rays are high-energy electrons that range in frequency of 10^{19}-10^{17} hertz. The primary sources of X-rays are the galactic core and our local Sun. X-rays are also released from radioactive nuclear matter. X-ray energy is so intense that it can penetrate and break down most forms of matter. Their ability to travel through matter is used in modern medicine by doctors to take pictures of the interior of the body (X-ray diagnostics). Overexposure to X-rays causes radiation sickness, in which the body breaks down and decomposes on the molecular level.

Ultraviolet radiation: UV radiation is composed of high-energy electrons that range in frequency from 10^{17}-10^{15}. The primary source of UV energy on Earth is the Sun. Sun lamps can create ultraviolet radiation as well. Ultra means beyond. Violet is a shade of purple. Beyond purple is blackness. Because of this, ultraviolet radiation is also known as Black light. Black light has profound impact upon matter, both organic and non-living. Black light ionizes matter, causing the electrons contained in the matter to become excited and/or released. Ion is another name for a 'free' electron. Black light's influence upon ions can cause:

- Photochemical processes (cause chemical reactions);
- Photoelectric reaction (cause some elements to produce electricity when exposed to Black light); and
- Fluorescence or iridescence (cause some elements to light up or illuminate).

Black Light has many potential benefits to hue-manity. It catalyzes the production of melanin throughout the body, particularly in the skin,sympathetic, and central nervous system. Black light harmonizes melatonin and seratonin secretions of the brain. Black light has antioxidant and bacteriological properties. It neutralizes toxic free radicals and eliminates bacteria and viruses from the body. Western medicine sometimes utilizes UV light to treat tuberculosis and infected skin legions because of this property. Black light also catalyzes the production of vitamin D, which is essential for healthy bone formation and maintenance. Black light is used by Western medicine for the treatment of rickets (bow legs) because of this quality. Black light accelerates the lymphatic and circulatory systems. It stimulates anti-body production, glandular activity and metabolic processes. It especially enhances the action of the lungs, heart, and sympathetic nervous system.

Optical light: Optical light is also known as visible light. This is the spectrum of light that can be seen by the human eye. The main source of visible light on planet Earth is the Sun. Compared to the other forms of electromagnetic energy, visible light is a very small spectrum. It ranges in frequency from 10^{15} - $10^{14.5}$ hertz. The full spectrum of visible light is called White light. White light is made of three primary colors: red, blue, and green light. These colored lights are considered primary because these color rays need to be equally present to produce white light. When two of these three colors are paired together, it will produce a secondary color.

Red + blue light = magenta

Green + red light = yellow

Blue + green light = cyan

Within the color spectrum, blue light is the highest frequency. It is approximately 10^{15} hertz. It is just below the ultraviolet spectrum. Green light is the mid-range of the optical light spectrum. Red light is the lowest of color frequencies. It resonates around $10^{14.5}$ hertz. Beyond its association with vision, visible light has profound effects upon the moods, physiological condition and sleep patterns of humans.

Infrared radiation: Infrared means *below red*. Infrared energy is invisible rays that have frequencies lower than visible red light. This band of energy is about five times larger than the spectrum of visible light. It ranges in frequency from $10^{14.5}$ hertz through 10^{11} hertz. Infrared radiation is the scientific name for heat rays. Heat rays elevate the temperature of matter, dehydrates matter, and excites matter into movement. Intense infrared radiation can cause matter to ignite, melt, vaporize, or combust. When fire consumes matter, infrared radiation is generated. The primary source of infrared heat on planet Earth is the Sun. Solar heat rays are invigorating to all life forms, but too much can cause dehydration and heat exhaustion. Pressure in the Earth's interior creates infrared radiation as well, and this heat is discharged through volcanic activity.

Radio waves: Radio waves are electromagnetic radiation emitted from rapidly vibrating metals. In nature, stars and planets are the primary sources of radio waves. For example, the iron core of planet Earth emits a radio signal due to the intense pressure and constant shifting of the Earth's mantle. Man can also generate radio waves by circulating an alternate current (AC electricity) through a metallic cone or rod (antennae). The electrical current causes the atoms in the antennae to vibrate rapidly. As the atoms vibrate, the antenna radiates radio waves that match the frequency of the electrical current.

Radio waves make up the largest band of energy within the electromagnetic spectrum. It ranges in frequency from 10^{11} through 10^3 hertz. Radio waves have three distinct forms. They are from highest to lowest frequency:

- Microwaves - Micro means "very small". These are the highest frequency of radio waves; therefore they have the smallest wavelength. Satellite and cellular phone communication is conducted over microwaves (10^{11} - 10^8 hertz).

- Short wave - The mid-range of radio frequencies (10^8 - 10^5 hertz). Television and FM radio frequencies are broadcast over short wave radio frequencies

- Long wave - The lowest range of radio waves (10^5 - 10^3 hertz). AM frequencies are broadcast over long wave radio frequencies.**Power frequencies:** Power frequencies are one of the lowest bands of the electromagnetic spectrum. They range in frequency from 10^3 hertz through 10^1 hertz. Power frequencies are commonly known as electricity. In nature, power frequencies discharge as lightening. Man generates these frequencies by chemical reaction (a battery cell) or rotating magnetic fields (generators). Electricity is the movement of electrons through a conductor. Unlike the rest of the electromagnetic spectrum, electricity cannot circulate through space or broadcast through the atmosphere. It can only discharge as lightening or a spark. Electrical frequencies are so low they must circulate through a conductive material such as metal or water. The passage of electricity through wire and modern electrical gadgets does create magnetic fields that permeate the atmosphere of the adjacent area. These magnetic fields are known as 'extra-low-frequency' (ELF) radiation.

Ferromagnetism: The phenomenon of magnetism is actually the lowest frequencies of the electromagnetic spectrum. Magnetism is a field of force that is created by the movement of electrons in a magnet. Natural magnet is an iron ore called magnetite. Man can create a magnet by coiling an iron rod with wire and passing an electric current through the coil. The field of force created by ferromagnetic substances either attracts or repels other magnetic substances and metals. Magnetism is closely associated with electricity and it shares the same frequencies as electrical energy. However, magnetism's range extends below power frequencies. Magnetic fields resonate from 10^3 hertz to 7 hertz. In nature, stars and planets usually contain magnetized metals, and as a result emit magnetic fields. For example, the iron core of the Earth has a magnetic field that resonates at 7.3 hertz. Below 7 hertz, no electromagnetic phenomena can be observed.

Sonic Energy

As stated, the **electromagnetic spectrum** is energy that consists of **moving atomic particles** (i.e. - electrons & protons). **The sonic spectrum** differs from the electromagnetic spectrum in that **the**

movement of matter (gasses, liquids, or solids) creates sonic energy as opposed to the movement of energy particles. Moreover, a medium is necessary to transfer sonic waves. In other words, sonic waves cannot travel through the vacuum of space as most frequencies of the electromagnetic spectrum can. There must be a medium of air, water, or earth for sonic vibrations to reverberate.

Sonic means *sound*, and is defined as a disturbance of matter to which the human ear is sensitive. The sonic spectrum is divided into three categories: *ultrasonic, audible, and infrasonic.*

Ultrasonic energy is sound that is above and beyond the human audible range. It is energy reverberating through the air that the human ear cannot hear. It ranges in frequency from 10^9 hertz, to 20,000 hertz. Western medicine uses high frequency ultrasonic energy to capture images of unborn fetuses in ultrasound diagnostic procedures. A dog whistle is an example of lower frequency ultrasonic energy. These whistles emit a sound that the human ear cannot detect. However, when one of these whistles is blown around a dog, it incites howling and other reactions because the pitch is within a dog's audible range.

Audible energy is what humans know and experience as sound. It ranges in frequency from 20,000 hertz to 20 hertz. Vibrating or moving matter creates waves of sound that ripple through the air. The waves are transmitted outward from their source, and when they enter the ear they produce the sensation of sound. The strumming of a guitar string is an excellent example.

Infrasonic energy is sound of such a low pitch; it is below the human audible range. There is no clearly defined lower limit of sonic frequencies below 20 hertz. Water turbulence, inaudible wind and air movement, and all forms of seismic activity (earthquakes) are considered infrasonic waves.

Matter

The densest of the three forms of energy, matter is considered to be vibrational energy that occupies space for a given time and has mass (weight). Matter is composed of 'frozen' protons and electrons. The particles are frozen in that they are immobilized and unable to travel as radiant energy. These immobile particles weave and intertwine with one another due to electromagnetic attraction. This attraction is also known as intermolecular force. Protons tend to carry an electrifying charge; electrons tend to carry a magnetic charge. The mutual attraction of these two particles causes them to bond together in atomic structures called molecules. Molecules then bond together and *materialize*.

There are two forms of matter, depending on how the molecules bond together: *amorphous* (without form) and *crystalline* (crystal-like).

Amorphous matter is composed of molecules that are bonded in a random, unorganized arrangement. The word 'amorphous' means *without form*. Since amorphous matter has a random molecular order, it usually does not produce things that naturally reflect measurable proportion, symmetry, balance, or organization. Sandstone, which is sand compressed into a rock, is an example of amorphous matter. Obsidian, which is hardened lava from a volcanic eruption, is another example of amorphous matter. Ice is an amorphous form of frozen water. In nature, all three of these materials are found in random arrangements, shapes and sizes.

What Is A Crystal?

In contrast to ice, a snowflake is a crystalline form of frozen water. 'Crystalline' means *crystal-like*, or *like a crystal*. Crystalline matter is composed of molecules that are organized and arranged in a consistent pattern. Crystalline molecules are naturally coordinated, synchronized, and balanced with one another. Any form of matter that has organized, coordinated and symmetrically arranged molecules is crystalline or crystal-like.

The significance of crystal-like matter is that the organized molecules are a reflection of a *unified energy field*. Probably the simplest way to describe a *unified energy field* is by making an analogy. Anybody who has attended an inspiring concert performance has experienced the electrical sensation of vibing in oneness with the singers, musicians, and the rest of the crowd. The shared harmonic vibration that is experienced by those present is a *unified energy field*. The shared vibe connects the individuals in attendance into one collective pulsating energy wave. Each person shares in the vibe, adds to the vibe, and harmonizes with the vibe.

Crystalline molecules come together in such a way that they generate and share a similar energy. The intermolecular force that bonds the molecules together is a coordinated, organized energy. It is as if a song is orchestrating the molecules into doing the same dance in unison with one another and within an equal distance from one another. In turn, each molecule adds to and harmonizes the collective energy field of the crystal.

This is important because the *unified energy field* of many forms of crystal yield energy potential. This means that certain crystals have the ability to produce or exchange energy. When molecules are congruent (arranged in harmonious alignment), they have the potential to freely share and exchange electrons with one another without decomposing. It is as if a cloud of free electrons permeates throughout the crystalline structure. In Physics, this cloud of ions within crystal-like matter is called **electron gas**. Ions in the electron gas move freely throughout the entire body of certain crystalline matter. This gives certain crystals the potential to:

- **Conduct** - Some crystals allow energy to travel through them, but offer some resistance or impedance to the energy flow.

- **Semi-conduct** - Certain crystals alternate between conducting an energy flow and insulating (blocking) an energy flow. This causes the energy flow to travel in a rhythmic pulse.

- **Super-conduct** - Certain crystals allow energy to travel through them without offering any resistance to the energy flow.

- **Resonate** - Some crystals amplify or add to energy circulating through them by resonating or vibrating in unison with the source of the energy.

The Phases Of Matter And Crystallization

Matter has three phases: gaseous, liquid, or solid. Take water for example. Depending on temperature and pressure, water can either be a:

- Cloud (gas);
- Body of water (liquid); or
- Solid (ice and snow).

All three phases of matter can have crystal-like organization of its internal molecules.

For example, **plasma** is a *crystal-like gas*. In Physics, plasma is defined as a gaseous body that has an organized, congruent molecular makeup. The molecules in plasma maintain an abundance of circulating free electrons. Because plasma has an abundance of free electrons, physicists call plasma *'ionized gas'*. *Ionized gas* is a remarkable super-conductor of electricity. The Earth's ionosphere, a thin band of charged electrons about 60 miles about the planet surface, is a body of plasma in nature. Neon gas tubes, often used in electronic advertising signs, are man-made plasma bodies. The gas in these sealed glass tubes acts like plasma in nature and conducts electricity. Neon plasma is used in ad signs because it discharges a fiery red glow when an electrical current passes through it.

Liquid crystals are fluids that have congruent, organized molecules and can conduct electricity. The liquid crystal display (LCD) watch is an example of a man-made liquid crystal. The 'mood ring' of the 1970's (the ring that changes color depending on the body temperature/mood of the wearer) is another. The crystal-like fluid within these modern gadgets is actually an organic compound derived from liquid cholesterol.

Clear Quartz As 'Crystal'

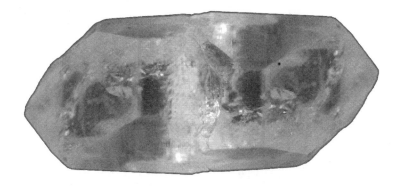

In spite of the fact that all three phases of matter can manifest in crystalline form, the most common perception of a crystal is a solid rock composed of organized, congruent molecules. There are several forms of rock specimens that fit this description. However, one stone in particular is commonly thought of as 'crystal' - clear quartz.

There are several reasons clear quartz is called 'crystal'. One reason is that the Greek word *Krystallos*, from which the word *crystal* is derived, means *'clear ice'*. Quartz crystal strongly resembles ice in that it is clear, translucent, and often has white wisps inside of it.

Another reason is that clear quartz is an abundant stone. It is found in varying forms throughout much of the world. Its elemental compound - silicon dioxide - constitutes 32% of the Earth's weight. That is the largest percentage of all elements. Iron constitutes the next largest percentage of the Earth's weight at 24%.

Yet another reason clear quartz is considered 'crystal' is the great energy potential of quartz. There is probably no other stone that has as many uses by humanity as quartz. Depending on the form of energy, quartz crystal can act as a conductor, semi-conductor, superconductor, or resonator of that energy. This is why quartz technology is the foundation of the silicon microchip computer and all forms of modern electronic communication. This is also why quartz technology is considered the premier tool in the emerging spiritual technology of the next millennium.

Properties Of Clear Quartz

Clear quartz crystal is a super-conductor of naturally occurring:

- High frequency cosmic radiation,
- Ultra-violet energy, and
- Geo-magnetic fields.

A super-conductor is any material that can transmit energy without offering resistance or impedance to the energy flow. The material must also be able to maintain stability and not break down while transmitting the energy.[2] The primary vibrations that are super-conducted by quartz include:

Cosmic radiation - This includes hard gamma, gamma, and x-rays. When these forms of radiation travel through space and penetrate Earth's atmosphere, they create super high-energy particle showers.

These particle showers rain down upon Earth and permeate the environment. Quartz super-conducts this cosmic energy. This makes quartz a valuable tool for attuning oneself with the high-energy cosmic radiation present in the environment.

Ultra-violet radiation - Also known as Black light, UV energy has profound impact upon matter, both organic and non-living. Black light causes photochemical processes, photoelectric reactions, fluorescence, and iridescence in various forms of matter. Quartz super-conducts UV energy; Black light passes through quartz unimpeded. Clear quartz allows UV light to pass through its molecular matrix without any resistance. In contrast, amorphous silica dioxide, commonly known as glass, blocks or insulates UV energy. Even though glass is made of the same two elements as quartz crystal, the unorganized molecular makeup of glass prevents Black light from passing through it. Quartz's ability to super-conduct Black light makes this stone a valuable tool for assisting oneself in assimilating UV radiation healthfully.

Geo-magnetic energy: Quartz super-conducts the geo-magnetic field of the Earth as well. The Earth exerts a mild magnetic field, the currents of which flows North/South. This geo-magnetic energy pulses or vibrates at 7.83 Hertz-per-second. Studies indicate that in areas where currents of geo-magnetic energy are intense, people grow stronger and are healthier. Where the Earth's magnetic energy is stifled; people tend to suffer greater incidences of debilitating disorders. Quartz crystal accumulates and super-conducts geo-magnetic energy, augmenting its presence in the surrounding environment.

Quartz Crystal is a conductor of:
- Visible light, and
- Infrared radiation

A conductor is a material that has the ability to transmit energy, but provides some resistance or impedance to the energy flow. Clear quartz conducts visible light and infrared light. In other words, clear quartz allows these forms of energy to travel through it; however, it impedes some of the light and infrared energy. This impedance manifests as reflection or refraction.

When visible and infrared light pass through clear quartz, it is either reflected or refracted. Clear quartz reflects light by scattering its rays in various directions. This gives quartz a luminescent halo when exposed to direct sunlight or bright light. Quartz refracts light by slowing the rays down and 'breaking' them up into a rainbow of separate color rays. Many crystals contain rainbows within their inclusions (inner realms), and some quartz will project rainbows like a prism when exposed to sunlight.

The reflection and refraction of light by clear quartz is the stone's resistance to the light energy. This resistance does two things:

1. It organizes, encodes and patterns the light waves that travel through it.

2. The impeded light energy is transformed into electrical discharges, giving quartz *photoelectric potential*, which is the ability to transform light into electricity.

Quartz's ability to organize and encode infrared light (heat rays) are utilized in the remote control technologies often found in modern entertainment systems. Infrared light is beamed through a quartz wafer within the remote control. The quartz then encodes the light with a signal. It is different electrical impulses channeled into the quartz that vary (changes) the signal. A silicon sensor on the television reads the signal and commands the entertainment system to change the channel, volume, etc.

The photoelectric potential of quartz is utilized in modern solar energy technologies. Silicon, the primary element in quartz (silica dioxide) is the key element in solar cells. Silicon discharges electrons when exposed to sunlight, and in the process transforms sunlight into electricity.

Quartz also has **pyroelectric potential**, or the ability to transform heat into energy.

Quartz discharges electrons when exposed to heat. This pyroelectric potential of quartz makes it the key component of digital thermometers and other heat sensing devices.

Clear Quartz is a resonator of:

- Radio waves

A resonator is a material that can change its internal frequency to match an external frequency. When that material matches the external frequency, the two vibrate in unison with one another. This state of mutual vibes is called *resonant affinity* (being in like vibration).

Quartz is a resonator of all forms of radio waves: microwave, long wave, and short wave. Crystal can amplify or add to a radio wave field by resonating or vibrating in oneness with the source of the radio signal.

In other words, when external radio waves enter quartz crystal, the crystal's unified energy field becomes one with the radio waves. In the process, the crystal amplifies and harmonizes the radio frequency with which it is in *resonant affinity*. During this process, the crystal and source of the radio waves are in *resonant affinity*. Television, radio, and most communication systems use this characteristic of quartz in selecting and isolating a chosen radio frequency so it can be transmitted and received without interference from other frequencies.

Quartz crystal is a semi-conductor of:

- Power frequencies.

A semiconductor is a material that alternates between conducting a flow of energy, and insulating the energy flow. This causes the energy flow to travel in a rhythmic pulse. Clear Quartz is a semi conductor of *power frequencies*, the electrical charges generated by chemical reaction (i.e. - battery) or rotating magnetic fields (generator). When electrical currents are passed through quartz, two things occur:

- The quartz discharges an intensified electrical field in a rhythmic pulse-like pattern. It is as if the quartz transforms the electrical current from a steady hum into an on/off rhythmic beating of a drum. This semi-conductive potential of quartz is the basis of the binary (0,1 / if: then) language of modern computer technology.

The quartz itself begins to physically vibrate. The rate of vibration depends on the strength and frequency of the electrical current. Several modern technologies are based on this feature of quartz. Thin slices of quartz are set to vibrate at precise rates; locking radios onto a specific station frequency or allowing multiple telephone calls to be transmitted over the same telephone cables.

A related feature of quartz is *piezoelectric potential*. *Piezo* means pressure. Quartz generates electricity when external pressure is applied. Physically squeezing and twisting quartz causes piezoelectric discharge. Bombarding quartz with sound vibrations causes piezoelectric discharge as well.

Practical applications for utilizing the super-conductive, semi-conductive, conductive, and resonating potential of clear quartz are explored in Part three - Aya.

Organic Matter is Crystalline

As stated, crystalline matter is any material that has coordinated and consistently organized molecules. **Organic** matter is **organized**, which makes it crystalline in nature. The word organic comes from the Latin root *organizare*, which means 'to arrange systematically'. *Organic* can have many meanings, depending on the context within which it is used. Organic usually refers to:

- Anything that naturally displays systematic coordination of its parts; and/or
- Anything dealing with the nature of plants and animals.

It is obvious that *organ-ic* shares the same root as *organ-ized*. All living organisms, plant and animal, are composed of organic matter. Therefore, based on the definition of crystalline matter, living organisms may be viewed as bio-crystalline beings - life forms that have bodies composed of organized and consistently ordered molecular structures.

In chemistry, organic matter is usually defined as a carbon-based material that displays systematic coordination of its molecular parts. Carbon is the primary building block of all living things on Earth. It is a complex element that has the ability to bond with most other elements. Some groupings of carbon-based molecules include:

- Hydrocarbons (combinations of carbon and hydrogen)
- Amino compounds (combinations of carbon and nitrogen)
- Organometallics (compounds of carbon and metals)
- Organosilicons (Silicone - compounds of carbon and silica)

Many forms of these carbon-based molecules are able to bond with one another in systematic and coordinated patterns. It is these molecules that tend to make up the living tissue of plants and animals. The fact that these molecules are organized means that they are crystalline. Moreover, the crystalline nature of organic molecules affords them energy potential. They are able to super-conduct, semi-conduct, conduct, and resonate various energies just like other crystalline materials. The crystalline molecules in a living body conduct the spirit life-force energy of the animating being.

The Hue-man Crystal: The Human Body as a Bio-crystalline Energy System

This has profound implications for how the human body can be viewed. From this perspective, the human body in its entirety is a:

- *Bio-crystalline energy system,* composed of
- *Bio-crystalline structures,* which in turn is composed of
- *Bio-crystalline molecules.*

A *system* is defined as an organized group that works together as a functional unit. A *bio-crystalline energy system* is a living (bio) body that has organized bio-crystalline structures working together as a unit. The bio-crystalline structures of the human body are its composite organs, tissues, bones, etc. These organic structures work together to maintain a balance of life force energy distributed throughout the entire bio-crystalline system (i.e. - the body).

A *bio-crystalline structure* is defined as the animated (bio) parts that are coordinated and arranged to form the whole body. These structures are composed of bio-crystalline molecules. These living molecules are arranged in an energy network that enables the *bio-crystalline structure* to conduct life force.

These structures are, from least dense to most dense:

- Blood
- Tissue (skin, muscle, and organs)
- Bone

Bio-crystalline molecules are carbon-based molecules that bond together in an organized pattern throughout *bio-crystalline structures.* Bio-crystalline molecules form a latticework, or energy network that facilitates reception and transmission of life force throughout bio-crystalline structures and the entire bio-crystalline energy system (the body).

There are three types of bio-crystalline molecules. They are in order of complexity:

- **Mineral salts,** which are ionic crystalline minerals often referred to as 'vitamins' ('living minerals).

- **Biopolymers,** which are organic molecules containing 'many (poly) life (bio) units (mer)'. Biopolymers are chains of carbon-based molecules that have bonded together. Hydrocarbons and amino compounds are the primary biopolymers in the body. Melanin is an example of a biopolymer.

- **DNA, or deoxyribonucleic acid,** which is a highly complex biopolymer composed of chains of less complex biopolymers. It is a giant crystalline molecule that is distinct from other biopolymers in that it contains encoded genetic information. This genetic information is inherited from parents, and is the blueprint design for building the entire biocrystalline energy system (the body).

Within the human body, these three bio-crystalline molecules are arranged in the form of various biocrystalline structures. The primary bio-crystalline structure is the cell. Each cell contains all three bio-crystalline molecules - mineral salts, biopolymers, and DNA. The DNA within each cell is the blueprint for the cell's design. Based on genetic instruction, cells differentiate or change from one another to perform specific tasks within the body. Cells, in turn group together to form more complex bio-crystalline structures.

To review:

- Mineral salts are the crystalline building blocks for biopolymers;
- Biopolymers are the crystalline building blocks for DNA;
- DNA is the crystalline building block for cells; and
- Cells are the crystalline building blocks for more complex biocrystalline structures: blood, bone, and tissue.
- Biocrystalline structures come together to form a complete biocrystalline energy system (body).

The perspective of the human body as a bio-crystalline system is not a new concept. Dr. Gabriel Cousins is one of the first within the medical profession to introduce this concept to the public. In 1986, he published **Spiritual Nutrition and the Rainbow Diet**, in which he asserts that the key to understanding how humans assimilate energy is to view the physical structure as a series of synchronized, oscillating liquid and solid crystals. The collective form-energy interaction of these crystalline structures creates the overall energy pattern for the body. He points out that organs, glands, nerves, cells, protein structures, and tissue salts operate with some degree of crystalline function.[3]

Randall Baer affirmed Cousin's perspective in **The Crystal Connection** (1987). He advocated that the perception of the human body as a multilevel, multidimensional bio-crystalline energy system be central to every level of health care.[4]

Melanin: The Key Bio-crystalline molecule

One of the most important biocrystalline molecules present in the human body is melanin. Melanin is a color pigment that is found in the skin and various internal organs. It is the molecule that gives people of color darkness of skin. The root for the word melanin comes from the Greek term 'mel' which means 'black'. 'Anin' comes from the related word 'amine', which usually refers to nitrogen based hydrocarbons (amino acids). Therefore, melanin literally means 'Black amino' and is a color pigment composed of a hydrocarbon chain that has various amino (nitrogen-based) compounds attached to it.

Melanin is a complex crystalline biopolymer with 'many' (poly) 'living' (bio) 'units' (mer). It is found in the nuclei of all cells, and concentrations of melanin may be found in the brain, pituitary & pineal glands, nervous system, heart, liver, muscles, gastrointestinal tract, skin, arteries, skin, eyes, auditory nerves, and gonads. Melanin is the central compound in the body that governs neurological and hormonal activity, as well as immune response.

The significance of melanin as a bio-crystalline molecule is that it displays the following energy potential:

Melanin functions as a superconductor within the body. A super-conductor is any material that can conduct energy current without offering any resistance to the energy flow. Melanin can transmit, transform, and transduce several frequencies of the electromagnetic spectrum without offering any resistance to the flow of that energy. Without losing its stability or cohesiveness, melanin has the potential for super-conducting a wide spectrum of vibrations, including:

- Cosmic radiation
- Ultra-violet radiation
- Infrared radiation
- Microwaves
- Radio waves
- Geo-magnetic energy

Melanin absorbs the aforementioned energies, and through super-conductivity transforms them into nutrition for the body. It does this without losing stability or dissipation of the transferred energy.

Melanin also super-conducts the internal neural impulses of the body. For example, the human ability to think and act instantaneously is possible because melanin super conducts electromagnetic nerve impulses to and from the brain simultaneously. In addition, melanin's super-conductivity gives it the potential to also act like a 'localized computer' and analyze a condition and initiate body response without reporting information to the brain.[5]

Melanin functions as a semiconductor of sound and heat energy. A semiconductor is a material that alternates between conducting an energy flow and insulating (blocking) the energy flow. In other words, melanin does insulate some energy contained in sound and heat waves; yet it also transforms some of the sound and heat energy into ionic nutrition for the body. Therefore, melanin is considered to have pyro-electric (generates electricity from heat) and piezo-electric (generates electricity from pressure) potential. Heat and the pressure of sound waves causes melanin to discharge electrical impulses. These electrical impulses are then transformed into ionic nutrition for the human body.

Melanin is a conductor of the body's ionic charge and acts as a battery for the body. A conductor is a material that has the ability to transmit energy, but it provides some resistance or impedance to the energy flow. Melanin conducts the electrochemical exchanges of the body's electrolytes. Electrolytes are ionically charged chemical solvents. Sodium and potassium are the two primary electrolytes within humans. As a conductor, melanin transforms electrochemical reactions into ionic nutrition for the body. In this regard, melanin is considered to have ionic potential. Ionic exchange and electrochemical processes govern all cellular nutrition, movement, reproduction, specialization, and permeability. As a conductor of the body's ionic energy, melanin plays a central role in **all** cellular activity.

Melanin is also considered a resonator. A resonator is a material that can change its internal frequency to match and vibrate in unison with an external frequency. In this regard, the human capacity to perceive external vibrations is governed by melanin. It is the primary crystalline molecule that permits vibrations to re-sound through the physical body. Melanin encodes and decodes external vibrations, processes them into mental information, and then transmits the information throughout the nervous system. The human capacity to perceive and react upon environmental vibrations is directly related to the amount of melanin present in the sensory organs and nervous system.

Melanin is also a resonator of visible light. That is why melanin is black in appearance - it absorbs all light energy and reflects none back. Brown and ruddy melanin pigment absorbs some light energy but reflects some back. As a resonator of visible light, melanin can absorb and transform light into ionic food for the body. In this regard, melanin is considered to have photoelectric potential (the ability to create electricity from light).

To summarize, melanin is the key bio-crystalline molecule of the Hue-man body. It acts as a super-conductor, semi-conductor, conductor, and resonator for the body's energy. Certainly, it is the melanin molecule that makes the Human Being a Human Crystal!

The Science of Super-Synergy

Comparing the energy potentials of clear quartz crystal and melanin, interesting similarities and contrasts exist. Clear Quartz crystal is a:

- Super-conductor of several forms of electromagnetic radiation
- Semi-conductor of power frequencies
- Conductor of visible light and infrared radiation
- Resonator of all forms of radio waves.

Melanin is a:

- Super-conductor of several forms of electromagnetic radiation
- A semiconductor of sound and heat energy
- Conductor of the body's ionic charge
- A resonator of visible light.

Recognizing the Universal Law that everything in creation is essentially vibrational energy - it is very significant that these two materials have such energy potential. A harmonious blending of the energy potential within these two multi-spectrum conductors would put a powerful force in the hands of Hue-manity.

Synergy means the combining of two things such that the combined effect is far greater than the sum of the effects if taken separately. For example, baking soda is a synergy of sodium and carbon. Baking soda is an excellent cleanser and deodorizer. It can do a far greater job cleaning and deodorizing than if either carbon or sodium were used independent of each other. The synergetic relationship of sodium and carbon as sodium bicarbonate is far greater than the sum effects of sodium or carbon used separately.

The synergistic application of melanin and quartz crystal are the primary tools in the spiritual technology for the new millennium. Combining these two multi-spectrum conductors is the way to empower people of color to harmonize and harness the full spectrum of vibrations within creation.

The Free Ion as the Physical Manifestation of Life Force

An electron "captured"
by molecular force

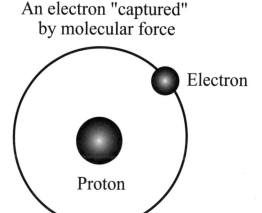

Electron

Proton

A Free Electron (Ion)

Model of Ion

There is one spectrum of energy in particular that the melanin/quartz synergy is a natural conductor and generator of - life force energy. Life force energy is Spirit - the animating awareness in all-living organisms. In terms of the Electro-magnetic spectrum, life force energy manifests as the negatively charged (passive) ion.

In the study of physics, the negatively charged ion is also known as a free electron, or hydrion (ionized hydrogen). Recall that atoms are composed of two primary particles: positively charged protons which form the atomic nucleus; and negatively charged electrons which orbit the nucleus. In terms of physics, an ion/electron that is free from molecular bond with a proton is free spirit energy.

The free ion is the nyama of the Dogon, the prana of ayruvedic teachings from India; it is the chi of Taoist philosophy from China. Ions are the life carrier in our air supply and are necessary in our growth process to build cells. The body cannot reproduce or repair one single cell without a supply of negative ions.

Not quite atoms, yet not quite radiant energy, ions are the first material manifestation of sunlight. The magnetic field of the Earth causes X-ray and ultra-violet light from the Sun to ionize; it transforms the ray of light into a passively charged electron. This photoelectric transformation occurs in the ionosphere, a highly charged particle field sixty miles above the Earth's surface. The ionosphere is the first band of the atmosphere separating the planet from outer space, and is considered the beginning of the atmosphere.

In the ionosphere, ions bind with one another, again due to the Earth's magnetic field. This causes the free electrons to condensate into ionized hydrogen atoms within the lowest strata of the ionosphere. These hydrogen ions thus bind with one another as the building blocks for all other atomic structures. Hydrogen ions, therefore, are the life-force materialization in its purist and finest form.

Below the ionosphere, ions circulate abundantly as charged sub-atomic particles. They are 'free' electrons that are not attached to atomic structures. Free ions are abundant around moving water - near a waterfall, babbling stream or ocean beach, also after a heavy rainfall.

However, many people of color are finding themselves in environments that are void of ions - toxic urban centers. A combination of pollution and artificial Electro-magnetic fields devitalize the free ions available in the air. Moreover, stressful urban lifestyles often stifle ionic activity within the body. Urban lifestyles often lead to 'free radicals' - toxins that rob cells of electrons - outnumbering free ions in the body. This sets the stage for all sorts of debilitating diseases.

Ions are essential to human vitality. The level of vitality and awareness of humans is directly related to the hydrogen ion level of the blood plasma. High levels of hydrogen ions in the blood plasma equate to high levels of vitality and awareness. Low levels of ions equate to low vitality and awareness. Ionic balance is vital to people of color.

Melanin maintains an ionic particle charge in its role as a low-voltage battery for the body. When the melanin ionic battery is charged, humans have energy. When toxins and stress drain humans, they have no energy. Music, sound, and motion excite ionic-particle circulation in melanin, and when melanin synergistically operates with quartz, its ability to produce free electrons increases greatly.

Throughout the ages, people of color have synergistically blended melanin and quartz - two powerful multi- spectrum conductors. The synergy of these multi-spectrum conductors was designed to generate ionic life force. This 'free' energy was the force behind the spiritual technology of antiquity. With these free ions, the ancients erected impressive monuments and temples, enhanced the topography of the planet, mastered amazing healing sciences, and produced magnificent cultural achievements. Before exploring the spiritual technology for the new millennium, it would be wise to know a little about how ancestral cultures used sacred stones.

Sankofa

Sankofa

Sankofa says 'Go Back and Fetch it! One must return and reclaim the past before one can advance into the future. Sankofa says to go back into the past and see that whenever African people achieved cultural greatness, sacred stones were integral and essential aspects of our cultural expression.

The idea of using melanin and sacred stones in a spiritual technology is not new. Africans have synergized these two multi-spectrum conductors throughout the Ages. Sankofa - Go back and fetch it! Sankofa - Return to the source! Go back and see that the Rocks of Ages have been the African foundation since the first Black nation. Go back!

SANKOFA

Sanfoka - The Stone Ages
A Historical Survey of
Hue-manity and Sacred Stones

This historical survey provides insight into the sacred stone science of ancient and contemporary African cultures. There are 6 themes that appear to express themselves across the cultures surveyed. From these themes, one can paint a clearer vision as to how People of Color have related to sacred stones throughout the ages.

- People of Color throughout time and space, have synergistically blended their melanin with sacred stones. The synergy usually involves adorning the body with sacred stone jewelry or implanting stones into cavities within the body.

- Sacred stones are central tools in the spiritual expression, religious rites and rituals of ancient cultures.

- Sacred stones are considered vehicles through which communion with ancestral spirits could occur.

- Clear Quartz Crystal is considered to be the Earthly home and throne of the One Most High (OMH) - The One God Creator.

- Meteorites, or Bet-Els are considered to be covenant stones, or stones through which the guidance and protection of the One Most High God (OMH) is made manifest.

- Our ancestors yielded legendary, mythical powers through combining the power of sacred stones with the power of their own melanin-rich biocrystalline systems.

This historical survey starts in the Nile Valley, the home of Africa's Classical civilizations of Kush (Ethiopia) and Kemet (Egypt). It then explores various cultures to the East and West of the Nile Valley; cultures that were seeded by the migrations of Kushites and Kemites out of the Nile Valley. Again, the intent is to paint a clear vision as to how People of Color have related to sacred stones throughout the ages.

KUSH

Herodotus, the Greek writer of the fifth century BCE, is considered by many to be the 'Father of History'. This is a false notion, because Herodotus himself clearly states that he studied with Egyptians who had chronicled the history of 330 reigning kings. However, much of the information that he chronicled is valuable, particularly about the regions of Egypt (Northern Nile Valley), Ethiopia (Southern Nile Valley), and Libya (Western and Sub-Saharan Africa).

Herodotus points out that:

- The Egyptians, Ethiopians, and Libyans were essentially the same race and practiced many of the same customs. They were the oldest race and their origins were the Upper Nile regions of Ethiopia.

- There are two distinct Ethiopians - the Eastern Ethiopians that live in the 'Fertile Crescent' of modern-day Iraq and Iran, as well as the Indian sub-continent of Asia. These Ethiopians were distinct from the Western Ethiopians of Africa. He describes both as having Black skin, however the African Ethiopians 'are the most wooly haired people on earth.' Herodotus says that the Eastern Ethiopians have straight hair due to their moist and humid climate.

- The Egyptians and Ethiopians established many colonies and were widely scattered throughout the world. These colonies included Colchis by the Black Sea. [1]

Herodotus also provides a great account of a Kushitic application of sacred stone science. In his recording of the Persian King Cambyses's campaign into Egypt and Nubia, he provides a Persian spy account of the 'Macrobion Ethiops' (Long-lived Ethiopians). Commenting on Ethiopian burial practices, the spies reported:

> Last of all, they [Cambyses' spies] were allowed to behold the coffins of the Ethiopians, which are made (according to report) of crystal, after the following fashion: When the dead body has been dried, either in the Egyptian, or in some other manner, they cover the whole with gypsum, and adorn it with painting until it is as like the living man as possible. Then they place the body in a crystal pillar that has been hollowed out to receive it, crystal being dug up in great abundance in their country and of a kind very easy to work. You may see the corpse through the pillar within which it lies; and it neither gives out any unpleasant odor, nor is it in any respect unseemly; yet there is no part that is not as plainly visible as if the body was bare. The next of kin keep the crystal pillar in their houses a full year from the time of the death, and give it the first fruits continually, and honor it with sacrifice. After the year is out they bear the pillar forth, and set it up near the town... [2]

This passage is significant, and when taken in context with a reference to Ethiopians by other 'classical' writers, has profound implications. Pliny the Elder, in his *Natural History*, says that the Ethiopians were originally known as the *Atlantae*. If this is the case, then the legendary *Atlantis* may not be beneath the Atlantic Ocean. More than likely *Atlantis* is beneath the seas of sand in the Sudan of Africa.

Much of what is known about *Atlantis* comes from the accounts of Aristotle and Solon, the well-known Greek philosophers. *Atlantis* is the 'Antediluvian' civilization, or the culture before 'The Great Flood'. Solon learned of *Atlantis* while studying with the priests of Sais - the school of priests within lower Kemet. These priests were of the most ancient of men. They considered Solon and his kindred 'children'.

> O Solon, Solon, you Hellenes are but children... As for the genealogies of yours, which you have recounted to us, Solon, they are no better than the tales of children; for in the first place; you remember one deluge only, whereas there were many of them.... [3]

Therefore, to get truer insight into *'Atlantis'*, Kemetic sources must be explored. Gerald Massey, in *Ancient Egypt: Light of the World* explores the language of the Nile Valley for a root of the Greek term *Atlantis*. He says that *Atlantis* is a compound word composed of two Kemetic terms:

Atl Antu. Atl is associated with water, and implies a limit or boundary marked by water. Massey says that *Antu* denotes a measure of land, nome, or mound. Therefore, Massey argues that the seven islands of *Atlantis* were the seven nomes of the Nile Valley, and canals and/or rivers defined the boundaries of these city-states. Massey continues:

> And among the nomes of Egypt we find the nome of the Prince of Annu; the nome of the Prince of Lower Egypt; the nome of Supti (Sut); the nome of Sanhutit (Heru); the nome of Sebek; the nome of Shu; the nome of Hapi. Here then, if anywhere on earth, we find a geographical prototype for the Atlantis that was lost in seven islands, according to the records kept by the astronomers, which are preserved in the mythography... [4]

Moreover, there is an account of a 'Great Deluge' in Kemetic tradition that clearly identifies the antediluvian geography. In the *Book of Coming Forth By Day* (Egyptian Book of the Dead), Chapter CLXXV recounts the Destruction of Mankind by Ra-Temu. Ra-Temu is dismayed at humanity because some rebels were plotting to overthrow his supremacy. He ascends above the Earth's surface in his 'Ark of a Million Years', and commanded Sekhet the heavenly lioness to unleash the waters of heaven and flood the planet. Sekhet does so, and the waters flood the seven nomes of mankind from Henensu in Upper Kemet (Edfu, the Greek Herakleopolis) all the way north to the nome of Lower Egypt. [5]

There is archeological evidence that supports that the Nile Valley has been completely inundated. For example, seashells have been unearthed in the sands right by the Great Pyramid of Giza. Moreover, the Sphinx of Giza shows definite signs of water erosion, even though it never rains in the Nile Valley. The pattern and position of the erosion indicates that the lower portion of the Sphinx - from the base of the neck down - was under water. [6]

If Upper and Lower Kemet were flooded out, the remnants of an antediluvian civilization would logically settle further South. The topography of the Nile Valley is such that the southern origins of the Nile are in highlands. The highlands were called 'Apta', and Mount Hetep by the Kemites. The Nile descends from Apta - particularly abruptly at three cataracts/water falls - and travels through the high-plains of the Sudan north through the low-plains of Egypt to the Mediterranean. Throughout the many deluges that were mentioned by the priests of Sais to Solon, the Ethiopian highlands have been the safe harbor place where a seed of hue-manity could survive and replenish the earth. These Ethiopian highlands and Sudanese plains were also the home of the Antediluvian kings, or the Atlanteans. More than likely, the ancient city-states of Napata and Meroe were two centers of Atlantean high culture.

The legends associated with Atlantean culture are fascinating. They truly had mastered a spiritual technology. It is legended that the Atlanteans had screens that showed pictures of events all around the world. It is legended that they had horse-less chariots that shot out white fire in front and red fire from its back. The Atlanteans also had air and space crafts of various sorts. It is said that the Atlanteans had globes of light that could be turned on and off automatically. Moreover, it is legended that the energy source for all of these various technologies was crystals that emitted an invisible radiation. [7]

It is legended that the Atlanteans had crystal light-braries, chambers in which information-encoded crystals were kept. The Atlanteans would learn lifetimes of information by simply holding these stones and allowing the information to download into their memory. Faces, animals, and other beings could be seen within the inclusions of these stones. It is legended that these stones were from the original home planet of the Atlanteans. These crystals are the original Rocks of Ages. [8]

Within this antediluvian culture that has been painted by the remnants of legends, the crystal burial pillars reported by Herodotus fit right in.

KEMET

When Herodotus visited Egypt, he traveled to Memphis, Heliopolis, and Thebes to speak with the priests of each of these nomes. In his accounts, it is clear that the learned class within Egypt was the priesthood, and that they served more than just a religious role in

Egyptian society. They were the calendar keepers, physicians, scribes/historians, counselors to royalty, and administrators of national affairs.

To become a priest in Kemet, one had to undergo 40 years of intense education. Concurrent with one's study, there was an initiation process designed to strengthen the moral character of the student. The core acts of the Kemetic initiation process was implanting and laying on the body crystals and sacred stones in ritualistic ceremonies.

This is the process described in-depth in the *'Book of Coming Forth By Day' (Egyptian Book of the Dead)*. Each chapter of the Book is a prayer to be recited by the priest during the initiation process, referred to as 'the making of a Shining One'. After each prayer is a rubric, which are instructions for the priests as to what to do while reciting the prayer. Some explicit chapters and rubrics referring to the implanting and laying on stones are as follows:

Chapter 'Of Transformation into A God'

"I have taken possession of the Ureret crown; Maat is in my body; her mouth is of turquoise and rock-crystal. My homestead is among the furrows which are lapis lazuli." (Clear allusion to stone implants).

Chapter of 'A Buckle of Carnelian'

"The triumphant Asar *Anu* saith: The Blood of Auset [carnelian], the enchantments of Auset, the power of Auset are a protection of this chief, it destroys what I abhor."

Rubric for 'A Buckle of Carnelian'

This chapter shall be said over a buckle of red jasper (carnelian) which has been dipped in water of ankham flowers and inlaid in sycamore wood, and has been placed on the neck of the shining one. If this chapter be inscribed upon it, shall become the power of Auset, and it shall protect him; and Heru, the son of Auset, shall rejoice when he sees it. No way shall be impassable to him, and one hand shall extend unto heaven, and the other unto earth. If this chapter be known he shall be among those who follow Asar Un-Nefer, triumphant. The gates of the underworld shall be opened onto him, and a homestead shall be given onto him, together with wheat and barley, in the Sekhet Aaru; and the followers of Heru who reap therein shall proclaim his name as one of the gods who are therein.

There is a similar chapter in the 'Book of Coming Forth...' entitled "The chapter of a Heart of Carnelian" with a similar rubric. They are so similar in fact; I do not include it in this historical survey, but only bring it to the reader's attention.

Rubric from 'Soul & Body'

"These words are to be said over a soul of gold inlaid with precious stones and placed on the breast of Asar." [9]

Wallace Budge, a so-called 'Egyptologist' who translated the *'Book of Coming Forth...'* has this to say about the rubrics as they relate to sacred stones:

"The Rubrics in the Book of the Dead show that the Egyptians considered it necessary to write certain 'hekau,' or 'words of power,' on certain kinds of stone, and this fact suggests that they attributed magical properties to such stones. Every stone used was believed to possess a certain magical power or influence which never failed to make operative when it was addressed in the proper manner, or when it was cut into a certain form, or had divine words of power cut upon it... [10]

The Kemites considered the *'Book of Coming Forth By Day'* as a guide for the Living into the Hollow Earth (Underworld) and for the Ever-Living (ancestors) into the Neter-world. The guide was put to practical application during the initiation process. The culminating phase of the ritual initiation, however, is not contained in the *'Book of Coming Forth by Day,'* but is a book in and of itself called *"The Ritual"* The final scene in *"The Ritual"* is called the *'Purification of Fire.'* Fearlessly using his newly gained powers to provide protection, the priestly initiate has to walk through a lake of water with fiery flames floating on top. Upon successful completion of the *'Purification of Fire,'* the initiate rises up and proclaims, *"I come from the lake of flame, from the lake of fire and from the field of flame, and I live."* He approaches 42 Masters of Maat, the Goddess of Truth, Justice, and Righteousness. A priest approaches the initiate and hands him a clear quartz crystal. A Master of Truth then asks, *"What have you been awarded?"* The initiate then utters *"A flame of fire and a pillar of crystal".*

Upon uttering this, the initiate has successfully completed the initiation process, the crystal acts as his diploma, and the 42 judges announce, "He is a spirit sufficiently advanced to join the ancient never-setting ones and become a fellow-citizen with them in the eternal city". [11]

By surveying the Books of *'Coming Forth By Day'* and *'The Ritual,'* it is clear that sacred stone science was an integral part of the initiation process in Kemet.

Considering the science of super-synergy, the purpose of the initiation rituals becomes evident. Kemetic High Priests spent their days blackening their bodies with sunlight to promote as much melanin production as possible. 'Egyptologist' call this act worshipping the Sun, and refer to Egyptian spirituality as 'Sun Worship'. In actuality, it is an act of increasing melanin production in the body.

At night, in the dark chambers of Kemetic temples, initiates participated in ceremonies in which super-synergistic stones were implanted, awarded, or placed upon initiates. In a universe where everything is vibration, they were empowering themselves with the super-synergistic tools needed to master creation - melanin and various crystals.

A Word about Mummification in Kemet

The purpose of mummification has remained a baffling mystery to 'Egyptologist'. Most have not been able to explain why priests would replace the body organs of deceased pharaohs and priests with sacred stones. Though initiates had gems implanted while alive, usually more stones were implanted during the process of mummification.

Moreover, the priests would wrap the 'karast' (Kemetic name for mummy) in such a way as to intentionally preserve the skin tissue. Egyptologists have attributed this to vanity on the part of Kemetic nobility. However, the science of super-synergy suggests that they were intentionally preserving their super-conductive skin melanin.

In 1986, the Senegalese scholar Cheikh Anta Diop conducted what he called the 'Melanin Dosage Test' on the mummified remains of Kemetic pharaohs. His test measured the amount of skin melanin present in the remains of pharaohs at the Cairo Museum. His tests showed that the amount of skin melanin within the mummified Kemetic corpses is notably high, even after thousands of years. [12]

The purpose of mummification is now clear. Preserved skin melanin and crystal implants empowers the karast to act as stabilized superconductor for the life-force spirit of the ancestral priesthood. These super-conducting karasts are literally immortal bodies through which ancestral nobility may move upon and influence earth while living in a heavenly celestial realm. Thousands of years ago, our ancestor's synergistic use of melanin and quartz created bodies, which even today acts as eternal superconductors for cosmic ancestral energy. 'Egyptologist' call them mummies.

The living Priesthood would use the karast as a communication system in which they could tune into the ancestral priesthood. Nur Akkh Amen (1993) explores this science in-depth in his powerful work, *The Ankh*. He points out that the sarcophagus in the King's Chamber of the Great Pyramid held the mummy of the God-King Khufu. Khufu's Karast was part of a high voltage circuit that allowed him to broadcast his consciousness from the *Anhket* (spirit world) through the Great Pyramid into this world. [13]

The *Khuti* (pyramids) and Tekhet (obelisks) of Kemet were constructed to harmoniously manipulate the electromagnetic (celestial) and gravitational (terrestrial) energies within the environment. They are literal antennas that broadcast celestial life force. Kemetic priest used these stone structures to collect, store, and project heavenly ancestral energy into their living environment. This is why mummies were kept in pyramids - They were considered broadcast stations moreso than tombs by the priests.

Herodotus' account about the Macrobian Ethiop's is now clearer as well. The practice of utilizing crystal coffins to store their mummified ancestors was a means of establishing an ancestral communication system through storing the super-conductive, immortal bodies of the ancestors in super-conductive crystal. Through these super-conductive channels, the ancestors could communicate clearly to their descendants.

Adornment of Sacred Stones in Kemet

Various amulets from dynastic times made of carnelian, malachite, lapis, and other precious stones.

In ancient artistic depictions, inscriptions, and in museum collections of today it is clear that the ancient Kemites adorned themselves from head to foot with sacred stones. Crowns of gold inlaid with Lapis Lazuli, Emerald, Agates, Jaspers are common. Several priestly adornments found are made from malachite, azurite, alabaster (calcite), fluorite, quartz of various colors, onyx, garnet, aquamarine and beryl of different colors, etc. There are even Kemetic sandals found which have precious stones embedded in them. In what ways did the priestly orders of the Nile Valley use these sacred stones? By studying Kemet's culture from a different angle, insight may be gained.

Israel

Origins of the Biblical Nation

Identifying the racial origins of the Biblical Hebrew Israelites is a complex, emotionally charged undertaking. Just as there are Christians and Muslims of every ethnicity, so to have Africans, Asians, Europeans, and Native Americans practiced Judaism throughout history. Being the oldest of the three 'World Religions', Judaic communities have been seeded throughout the earth for close to 3000 years. There are historical accounts of African, European, and Asiatic Judaic communities existing at the very same time in history; and each group claims direct descent from the original nation of Israel.

However, a careful examination of Biblical history reveals that the ethnic roots of the Hebrew Israelites are African. There are two main keys in the Old Testament that reveals the African origins of Israel: Abraham's roots in the Fertile Crescent, and Moses' sojourn in Egypt.

The Anu

Concerning Abraham, it was mentioned that Herodotus described two distinct Ethiopians - Eastern Ethiopians that live in the 'Fertile Crescent' of Asia; and Western Ethiopians of Africa. The most notable city-states of the Eastern Ethiopians were Sumar (the biblical Shinar), Ur, Elam, Uruk, Chaldea, Kish, Nippur, Susa, and Lagash. These Afro-Asiatic cultures were loosely interrelated nomes situated in today's Jordan, Syria, Iraq, and Iran. At times they were a unified federation; at other times they were in conflict and at war with one another. One common trait among them was their name for themselves: The Anu, "The Black-Headed People".

> ...The Sumarians were dominant in Lower Mesopotamia. This folk, who called themselves "the black headed people" and their land Sumar, were neither Semites nor Aryans and their language, in which many text are now available, was neither Semitic nor Indo-European.". [15]

The *Anu* recognized the common ancestry of the different city-states, and viewed themselves collectively as the children of the Heavenly Father *An*. For example, when the King and Founder of the Third Dynasty of Uruk, *Ishakku Lugalzagissi* united the whole fertile crescent, he inscribed the following prayer on a temple in Nippur:

> "...May Enlil king of the countries prefer my prayer before his dear father An. May he add life to my life; cause the country to rest at peace with me. Folk as numerous as scented herbs may bestow on me with open hand; guide for me the flock of An; look benevolently for me upon the land. Let the gods not change the good destiny that they have assigned to me. Shepherd, leader let me be forever." [16]

It should be noted that in Kemet, *An* is the throne name of *Ra*. The *Anu*, as with their Kemetic brethren, applied a sacred stone science that involved synergistically combining their melanin with crystals, metals, and gems.

The nobility of the *Anu* treasured gold and lapis lazuli, and most in the noble family wore headdress made out of gold and lapis.

There is an account of a governor of Lagash named Gudea who used some mythically powerful sacred stone science to initiate a renaissance of Sumarian influence and culture. In 2180 BCE, a group of Caucasian nomads called the Gutians overran the Fertile Crescent and ruled through 2070 BCE. The Sumarians regained supremacy over the region because of Gudea's divinely inspired work. In a dream, it was revealed to him that he was to reconstruct a temple for Anunnu in Lagash. Gudea recounted that "In the dream a man that shone like the heaven and was joyful like the earth - from the crown of his head he was a god... he commanded to build a house; his meaning I did not understand".

Then, a warrior appeared in his dream and held up a tablet of Lapis Lazuli. On the tablet was inscribed the plans for a temple. Without delay, Gudea proceeded to construct the temple, he himself setting the first stone. He fitted the temple with cedar wood and various sacred stones. When completed, "The Holy Temple rising from earth to heaven...shone in the brilliance of heaven with radiant light... It illuminated the country". [17]

It was as if Anunnu's temple had broadcast a vibration that established a unified energy field within the Fertile Crescent. This energy field connected the *Anu* with *An* the Heavenly Father and with each other. They were able to unite, overcome the Gutians, and The Third Dynasty of Ur was established. Its first King was *Ur-Nammu "King of Sumar and Akkad"*.

There is another account of Sumarian sacred stone science, this one with the priesthood at Nippur - The *Ibri*. Nippur was the Holy Land or religious city within the nation of Sumar. Nippur is the city to which the 'Flock of Anu' traditionally made a pilgrimage to honor *An*. The Ibri were high priest who established and maintained the central temple of

An. The primary responsibilities of the Ibri were to be the 'Shepherds of the Flock of An'; as well as be guardians and diviners of 'the stones that whisper". [18]

Although the inscriptions which mention the 'Stones that Whisper' do not identify exactly which sacred stones were the ones maintained at the temple, more than likely they were clear quartz crystals. A clue which indicates that they were clear quartz is the symbol the priesthood chose to represent themselves - the hexagram or six-pointed star.

Clear quartz always grows on a six-sided axis, has six distinct faces, and the energy dynamic within the stone creates two interlocking triangles. It would follow that if the primary responsibility of the Ibri were to maintain 'the stones that whisper', that they would employ a symbol that embodies the energy within those stones. This would suggest that the priestly Ibri are the Sumarian root of Judaism's Abraham and Islam's Ibrihim.

According to biblical history, Abram the Patriarch of Israel 'was brought out of Ur and Chaldea' and named Abraham. He left because of a 'famine' and traveled into the Nile Valley. Historians date Abram's departure at around 1900 BCE This is a critical timeframe for the *Anu* in the Fertile Crescent.

Even though the work of Gudea allowed the *Anu* to defeat the Gutians and regain governance of the Fertile Crescent, it did not stop the raids and incursions of the Northern Caucasian Nomads. In fact, the frequency of raids intensified greatly between 2000-1900 BCE. Frequent incursions created a destabilized social climate and disrupted the agricultural growing cycles. Thus, there was a weakened defense and a lack of resources. The Sumarians called these disruptive raiders the 'Mar-tu':

> The Mar-tu, who know no grain... The Mar-tu who know no house or town, the boors of the mountains... The Mar-tu who does not bend (to cultivate land), who eats raw meat, who has no house during his lifetime, who is not buried after his death.

The Sumarian Mar-tu are the biblical Amorites, 'The Mountain Dwellers', whom it was foretold to Abram that 'thy seed shall be a stranger in a land that is not theirs... for the iniquity of the Amorites is not yet full' (Gen., Chap. 15). 1900 BCE is a peak timeframe of the nomadic incursions. In such an unstable climate, the Ibri were forced to migrate with their whispering stones southwest into the Nile Valley. Thus, you have 'Ibri-him' the Shepherds (Abraham) migrating into Egypt.

One reason that they sought refuge to the Southwest is because the incursions were coming from the Northeast. However, a more significant reason is that the Ibri had 'family' in the Nile Valley.

The *Anu* originated in the highlands of the Upper Nile region where the Blue and White Nile begin. They migrated east and settled in the Fertile Crescent, but they followed the Nile North and established colonies in Upper and Lower Egypt as well. Their cities bore their name - *An*. *An* is the Biblical On ('The Stone') and the Greek *Heliopolis* ('City of the Sun'). *An* in Lower Kemet is situated next to modern Cairo. *An* in Upper Kemet was the capital of the 4th Upper Egyptian nome, and is modern Armant, the Greek *Hermonthis*, Coptic *Ermont*, and Kemetic *Anu-Montu*. It is located approximately 20 kilometers south of Ipet Isut (Luxor/Thebes).

It would follow that once in the Nile Valley, the *'Ibri'* - the Biblical Abraham - sought refuge with their sister order the *Anu* at *An*. Moreover, *On* is not a Hebrew equivalent of the Kemetic *An*, which means 'Fish'. *On* means 'stone' in Hebrew, suggesting that the 'Ibri' deposited 'the Stones that Whisper' there.

From Abraham through Jesus, *On* appears to be the central focus of Israelite interaction with the nation of Kemet. When Joseph sojourned in Kemet, he married the daughter of the High Priest at *On* - Asenath who bore him two sons, Manasseh and Ephraim.

Tradition has it that Moses, the 'Lawgiver' of Israel, was a priest from *On*. The Old Testament states that 'Moses was learned in all of the ways of the Egyptians'. Apion, a dispersed Israelite who lived during Greek domination of the Eastern Mediterranean, states: "I have heard of the ancient men of Egypt, that Moses was of Heliopolis, and that he thought himself obliged to follow the customs of his forefathers..."

Apion argues that the Kemetic Priests of his time viewed Israel as a kindred nation and that the Israelites were originally Kemites. Israel was politically and militarily allied to Kemet, and "swore by God, the Maker of the Heaven and Earth and Sea to bear no good will to any foreigner, and particularly to none of the Greeks."[20]

Manetho says "he was by birth of Heliopolis and his name was Osarsiph, from Osyris the god of Heliopolis, but that he changed his name and called himself Moses."

Tacitus states: "Many consider them [Israel] to be the progeny of the Aethiopians who were impelled by fear, and the hatred manifested against them, to change their settlements in the reign of King Kepheus (Ma-Shu)..." Tacitus' "Ma-Shu" is usually associated with the biblical Moses.

Celsus, whom Gerald Massey called "the well informed Roman", says that the "Jews were a tribe of Egyptians who revolted from the established religion."

Polemo, in his first book of his Egyptian histories, says "In the reign of Apis, the son of Pharonaeus, a portion of the Egyptian army deserted from Egypt and took up their habitation in that part of Syria which is called Palestine, not far from Arabia".

Within the Nile Valley during the time of Moses, The Priests of *An* were engaged in a battle with the Setians over the nature of government in the region. The Priests of *An* and their brethren, the *Ibri*, ruled by counsel, reason, justness, and righteous example in the name of Ra and Isis (Is-ra-el), and led all who followed on a path of Self-Empowerment. The Pharaohs of the Amon-Ra order (V-XII Dynasties, as well as XVIII-XXXth Dynasties) were the High Priest Kings. As a Priest-King, the rulers governed in counsel, and could not make decisions without approval of the majority of the priests.

Diodorus Siculus describes the relationship of the Amon-Ra priesthood and the High Priest King:

> The priests who are employed in the service of the gods of Meroe exercised the greatest authority. For they could whensoever they pleased, send a messenger to the king commanding him in the name of the god to

put himself to death...[and]...no king ever dared to resist the priestly orders, but observed their dictates without force or compulsion".

The Setians

This put the Priesthood of Ra (The Israelites) at odds with the Rebel God Set, his Regents and Priesthood. The Setians ruled through enslavement, ignorance, and brutality, and each successive Setian King wanted absolute authority over all of Hue-manity.

The Setian Priesthood is an ancient order. Within Kemet, their center of power was in the 19th nome. Per-medjed was their capital and central temple (Coptic Pemdje, Arabic el-Bahnasa). According to Kemetic cosmology, the Setians were once noble, and ruled a fabled land called Ta-Seti - Land of the Bow. Ta-Seti was situated in the Sudan and Southern Nile regions. However, over time Set's character grew wicked, and depending on the age of the cosmology, Set is depicted in one of three ways:

Rebelling against Ra his Heavenly Father: In this version of the mythic drama, Heru and Set are twins. Set is the first-born; however, Set has a sinister taint to his character and embodies darkness, envy, jealousy. Set leads an army of Sebau serpents and Apap reptiles in a rebellion of Ra's authority on Earth.

Heru embodies righteousness, the light, the right, truth, and justice. Heru comes in the role of 'Heru Behutet' or Heru-Khuti from Behutet. 'Behutet' is the 'City of Heru' - modern day Edfu - in these predynastic times. As Heru-Khuti, he is the Sun God of the Two-Horizons who defends and upholds the Council of Ra on Earth. Heru Behutet flew the golden winged disk of Ra into battle. When Heru flew the disk into battle, it would blind, deafen, and stupefy his enemies. With the flying disk of Ra, Heru slaughtered the Sebau by the hundreds. The Sebau were slaughtered for conspiring with Set to fight against Ra's authority. After the first slaughter, Heru flew to the Ark of Ra to encourage Ra to sail low to Earth so that he may view the bloodied battlefields. Ra did so, and was very pleased with Heru-Behutet.

Heru in turn committed two more slaughters of the Sebau Serpents. When Set saw what Heru had done to his conspirators, he confronted Heru. Heru lanced Set in the neck with one of his spears, then marched Set to Ra. Ra said that Heru and Auset can do whatever they wanted to do with Set. Heru slaughtered Set, cut off his head, mounted it and his headless body on a spear, and paraded through the land showing off the defeated Rebel-God.

After these events, the spirit of Set transformed into a serpent and hid in a hole in the ground. Heru took a pole and stuck it in the hole. Upon the pole he put his emblem, a Hawk's Head or winged disk. This bound Set in the hole for the rest of the Age, and established Heru as the unchallenged Living Sun God and King on Earth.

Engaging in perpetual warfare against his brother Heru; In this form of the drama, Set is the First-born of the *Khem-Anu (The 8 celestial ancestors of hue-manity)* and Heru Ur - Heru the Elder - is the last-born. Heru is considered the Elder because as the eighth child of Ra, he stayed in Nut's celestial womb and gestated the longest term. Set is recognized as the first-born of the *Khem-Anu*, but it is said that Set violently and impulsively jumped out of his mother Nut's womb prematurely. Because of this violent and impulsive act, Ra awarded the title of 'Elder' to Heru. Along with the title came the Eye of Ra and the Crown of Kingship of Earth.

Set was outraged that his birthright had been given away. This caused Set to challenge Heru to a battle, which took on many forms. At one point, they are hippopotamuses battling underwater. At the most dramatic point, Set attempts to sodomize Heru by violating his rectum and releasing his sperm into Heru's body.

Heru was able to prevent the seed from entering his body by catching it in his hand. He ran to show Auset, who quickly cut off his hand. After regenerating a new hand for Heru, Auset came up with the plan to sprinkle Heru's sperm onto Set's sacred lettuce so that Heru's seed would be ingested by Set. They did. That evening, Set ate Heru's sperm, causing Heru's power to defile Set internally.

Set still did not accept defeat, and continued to fight against Heru. This continued aggression was against the laws established by Ra, so he charged Set with violating Divine Law. Heru was finally able to bind Set in chains and present him to Ra as a criminal and prisoner. Set is then banished to the desert regions and is transformed into Anpu the Black Jackal. As Set-Anup, Set becomes associated with chaos, burning winds, drought, darkness, barrenness, infertility, and death.

Killing his brother Asar and abdicating his throne: In this form of the mythos, Geb is the Earthly father. When he was ready to ascend into heaven, he gave his throne to Asar (Osiris). When Asar became King of Earth, he committed himself to teaching culture and civilization to hue-manity. He advocated vegetarianism and taught the science and technology of agriculture. Asar was said to have established many temples and taught hue-manity in the ways of paying homage to the One God in Her many forms. Asar refined the way of living and increased the comforts within the Nile Valley during his reign. He ruled as a righteous King and Enforcer of Maat.

Of course his brother Set grew envious and jealous of Asar's reign as a prosperous King. He conspired against the King and through an elaborate scheme trapped Asar in a sarcophagus. Set took Asar away, assassinated him and then dismembered his body into 14 pieces. Set scattered Asar's body parts throughout the Nile Valley, then assumed the throne as King of Earth.

Auset, the wife of Ausar and Queen of the Land, wailed and mourned. She searched the land and was able to recover all of Asar's body parts. With the help of Nebhut, Auset reassembled the King. Auset then performed a magical act with Asar's body and conceived a son - Heru. Heru came of age and was viewed as a resurrection or reincarnation of his father. Heru avenged Set for his father's death and reclaimed the throne of Earth for his father.

The Setians Hire Foreign Hyksos Invaders to Control Kemet

The priesthood of Set migrated north just as the priesthood of *Anu/Amen-ra* did. They established temples in Ta-Meri (Land of the Virgin; another name of Kemet), and coexisted with the other priesthoods from the first through the twelfth dynasties. From the Twelfth through the Eighteenth dynasties however, the Setians and the Priests of Ra were engaged in a power struggle within the Nile Valley as to the nature of government. By 1700 BCE, Set and the Setians became a detested and despised group by the Kemites. As Wallace Budge points out, "the popularity of his cult suffered greatly at this period because he was associated with the occupation of Northern Egypt by the Hyksos, who identified him with certain Semitic, Syrian gods."

Manetho states that the rulers of the fifteenth dynasty were 'six foreign from Phoenicia, who seized Memphis; who also founded a town in the Sethroite nome, from which as a base they subdued Egypt.'

The Pharaoh who oppressed the Biblical Children of Israel was a Setian. More than likely, he was the Hyksos King Apepa (also known as Apis), who made Set the national god of the Delta and established a temple for him at Het-uart (Avaris) around 1550 BCE. The Hyksos were nomadic invaders from Eurasia. Apepa was a Hyksos who the Setian Priesthood enthroned. He was notoriously cruel to the indigenous Kemites, and openly hostile to the Amon-Ra priesthood, who during his reign was centered in Thebes to the South.

All of this points to the fact that the original nation of Israel was ethnically, culturally, and socially African. Israel was not originally a Semitic, non-African ethnic group, but a federation of the Ibri and the Amon-Ra order. This perspective affirms that the Biblical Israelites were culturally, politically, and spiritually aligned with the indigenous Africans of the Nile Valley. This counters the popular view of the Biblical Israelites - that they were nomadic Semites who had a different racial identity from the Kemites.

Moreover, the Old Testament account of Israel's sojourn into the Nile Valley clearly affirms this perspective. In Genesis 47, when Jacob moves to Egypt and is presented to Pharaoh by his son Joseph (who married the daughter of the priest from *An*), the leader of Kemet says:

"Thy father and thy brethren are like unto thee: The land of Egypt is before thee; in the best of the land make thy father and brethren to dwell."

It then states that "... Joseph [son of Jacob] placed his father and his brethren, and gave them a possession in the land of Egypt, in the land of Rameses, as Pharaoh had commanded...".

Rameses would not have invited nomadic Semites into the Nile Valley and have given them the best of land!

There is an archaeological site in the 13th nome of Lower Egypt - the nome in which *An* is the capitol - called "Tell El Yahudiya", or 'The Mound of the Jews'. At "Tell el Yahudiya" there are remains of two temples: one of Rameses II and the other of Rameses III. This may have been 'the best of land' offered the Ibri upon their return to Kemet.

In Exodus, Chapter One, it states that "there arose a new king over Egypt, which knew not Joseph." This was the Hyksos King, who "said onto his people, Behold, the people of the children of Israel are more and mightier than we". [27]

This affirms that the Pharaoh in the Bible who oppressed Israel and worked them as slaves was an outnumbered foreign dominator who had conquered the Delta region of the Nile. Moses, then, is actually an African freedom fighter.

Ahmes I is the Biblical Moses

The biblical Moses is probably Ah-moses I (a.k.a. Yahmose I or Aahemes I), the founder of the 18th Dynasty and New Kingdom of Kemet. Ah-moses reigned from 1539-1514 BCE. Ah-moses I was from the royal family that ruled Upper and Lower Kemet before the Hyksos occupation - the last Pharaohs of the XIV dynasty (circa 1786 BCE). These Pharaohs were also High Priest Kings of the Amon-Ra order, and their base of power was Thebes in Upper Kemet and *An* in Lower Kemet. Ahmes I was the first indigenous Pharaoh of this line to expel the Hyksos and re-establish power to the Priesthood of Amen-Ra in Upper and Lower Kemet. He defeated the Setian Pharaoh Apepa (Apophis), destroyed Set's temple of worship at Avaris (Tanis in the Delta), and actually extended Kemet's northern border into Palestine, taking control of Sharuhen and Tell el'Ajull (Ancient Gaza).

Appointed and anointed by the Amen-Ra priesthood, Ahmes I was involved in military activity attributed to the Biblical Moses - battling the incursions of nomadic mountain dwellers from the North and east. Not only did Ahmes I overthrow an oppressive Pharaoh and led a military campaigns into the biblical "Palestine", he did something else associated with the Biblical Moses. His wife was an Ethiopian Princess - the beautiful Nefartari. Nefartari was a Napatan/Theban princess and daughter of the Napatan King. She is described as 'a black Ethiopian princess'.

The union of Ahmose and Nefartari was a very important one - it re-united the royal families of Sumar, Kemet, and Kush. Details of how Moses married an Ethiopian woman are contained in an obscure Hebrew manuscript entitled "The Upright Or Correct Record", also known as the "Book of Jasher". The Book of Jasher also affirms that Moses was a Pharaoh who wore the crown of Upper Egypt.

Despite its obscurity, the "Book of Jasher" actually has two Old Testament references. The first is by Joshua, who called for the Sun to stand still during his battle against the Five Amorite Kings. When the Sun stood still and granted victory for Israel, Joshua exclaimed, "Is this not written in the Book of Jasher?"

The second biblical reference is in II Samuel, in which he speaks of David's lamentation of Saul's passing. In eulogizing Saul's life, David laments "Also he bade them teach the children of Judah the use of the bow, behold it is written in the Book of Jasher". [28]

The Judaic Historian Josephus says of the Book of Jasher: "That by this book are to be understood certain records kept in some safe place on purpose, giving an account of what happened among the Hebrews from year to year, and called Jasher, or the Upright, on account of the fidelity of the annals". [29]

The Book of Jasher contains an incredible account of Moses. As in the Old Testament, it states that Moses grew up in the King's House. It recounts his travels in Goshen, and his petitions to Pharaoh on behalf of the Israelites. It also recounts Moses slaying an Egyptian in defense of an Israelite, and that he had to flee the Lower Nile Valley. However, unlike the Old Testament, *The Upright and Correct Record* reveals that Moses fled to Kush, and ruled over Kush for 40 years.

When Moses arrived in Kush, he encountered the army of King Kikianus, [30] who was returning from battling 'Aram of the East' in Asia. Aram was a King who was subjected to Kikianus, but had rebelled. Aram then allied himself with the Amorites and waged war upon Kush. Kikianus had re-subjugated Aram and was returning from this battle. However, while he was gone, a corrupt priest named Balaam had usurped his power and erected huge, fortified walls around Kush ('Kush' is probably Napata or Meroe). The 'Magician King' also had deep trenches filled with poisonous serpents surrounding the gates of the town. King Kikianus was besieging his own kingdom when Moses encountered him and his troops. Kikanus lost several hundred men, and was unsuccessful for a span of nine years. During this time however, Moses had allied himself with the King and was helping him regain governance of Kush.

Then, Kikianus became ill and passed away. At that point, Moses earned Kingship of Kush by coming up with the following plan:

> And all the children spoke together in the presence of the king, saying, give us counsel that we may see what is to be done to this city.

> For it is now nine years that we have been besieging round about the city, and have not seen our children and our wives.

> So the king [Moses] answered them, saying, if you will hearken to my voice in all that I shall command you, then will the Lord give the city into our hands and we subdue it.

For if we fight with them as in the former battle which we had with him before the death of Kikianus, many of us will fall down wounded as before.

Now therefore behold here is counsel for you in this matter; if you will hearken to my voice, then will the city be delivered into our hands.

So all the forces answered the king, saying, all that our lord shall command that will we do.

And Moses said unto them, pass through and proclaim a voice in the whole camp unto all the people, saying,

Thus says the king, go into the forest and bring with you of the young ones of the stork, each man a young one in his hand.

And any person transgressing the word of the king, who shall not bring his young one, he shall die, and the king will take all belonging to him.

And when you shall bring them they shall be in your keeping, you shall rear them until they grow up, and you shall teach them to dart upon, as is the way of the young ones of the hawk.

So all the children of Cush heard the words of Moses, and they rose up and caused a proclamation to be issued throughout the camp saying,

Unto you, all the children of Cush, the king's order is, that you go all together to the forest, and catch there the young storks each man his young one in his hand, and you shall bring them home.

And any person violating this order of the king shall die, and the king will take all that belongs to him.

And all the people did so, and they went out to the wood and they climbed the fir trees and caught, each man a young one in his hand, all the young of the storks, and they brought them into the desert and reared them by order of the king, and they taught them to dart upon, similar to the young hawks.

And after the young storks were reared, the king ordered them to be hungered for three days, and all the people did so.

And on the third day, the king said unto them, strengthen yourselves and become valiant men, and each man his armor and gird on his sword upon him, and ride each man his horse and take each his young stork in his hand.

And we will rise up and fight against the city at the place where the serpents are; and all the people did as the king had ordered.

And they took each man his young one in his hand, and they went away, and when they came to the place of the serpents the king said to them, send forth each man his young stork upon the serpents.

The storks swooped down into the pit and devoured the serpents, allowing the army of Kikianus to enter Cush. They retook the city and expelled Balaam. Upon doing so,

"all the people of Cush issued a proclamation on that day, saying, every man must give something to Moses of what is in his possession.

And they spread out a sheet upon the heap, and every man cast into it something of what he had, one a gold ear ring and the other a coin.

Also of onyx stones, bdellium, pearls and marble did the children of Cush cast unto Moses upon the heap also silver and gold in great abundance.

And Moses took all the silver and gold, all the vessels, and tile bdellium and onyx stones, which all the children of Cush had given to him, and he placed them amongst his treasures.... **And they placed the royal crown upon his head,** and they gave him for a wife Adoniah the Cushite Queen, wife of Kikianus....

And Moses reigned over the children of Cush on that day, in the place of Kikianus king of Cush... And the Lord granted Moses favor and grace in the eyes of all the children of Cush, the children of Cush loved him exceedingly, so Moses was favored by the Lord and by men... [30]

The royal crown of Moses was probably the Crown of the Upper Nile, and he was the ruler of the indigenous Kemites in Southern Kemet and Northern Nubia - placing him in opposition to the Setian Pharaoh who was in control of the Northern Nile delta region.

While King, Moses continued Kikianus' battles with Aram of the East and the Amorite Kings. Since Ah-Moses was an Ibri, he considered the Land of the East the 'Promised Land' because it was the land of his forefathers who had to flee into Africa on account of Amorite invasions.

African-Centered Chronology
From Anu to Ahmes:
The Kemetic version of Noah to Moses

This chronology is a summary of Kemetic cosmology and the history of the Nile Valley civilization.

26,000 BCE - The Anu, "The Black-Headed", also known as the "Fish People" found Ta-Neter in the highlands of the Great Lakes region of modern day Uganda, Tanzania, Kenya, and Rwanda. Ta-Neter is the 'Land of the Gods'. The Anu are the biblical Noah.

19,000 BCE - The Anu follow the White Nile North and found the nation of Ta-Seti, the 'Land of the Bow'. Ta-Seti was situated in the plains of Sudan and the highlands of the African Horn. The most powerful priesthood in this nation was the Setians. The city-states of Meroe and Napata are found in the land of Ta-Seti. This is the kingdom of the biblical Nimrod, the 'Strong' son of Kush and grandson of Noah. Nimrod is the mighty hunter that goes forth with the bow 'before the Lord'.

13,000 BCE - The Anu continue to follow the Nile North and establish Ta-Meri 'Land of the Virgin'. Ta-Meri is upper and lower Kemet from Aswan north to the Delta. The city-states of An (Heliopolis), Annu (Hermopolis), and Abdu (Abydos) are the most ancient of nomes in Ta-Meri.

6,000 BCE - The Anu begin to settle in the Fertile Crescent of Asia. They founded the city-states of Ur, Urak, Chaldea, Sumar, Lagash, Nippur, and Mohenjo Daro.

3100 BCE Menes unites the various city-states of Ta-Meri, initiating the 1st Dynasty of Kemet.

2000 BCE - The Mar-tu - the biblical Amorites - descend from the Caucasus Mountains and invades Anu settlements in and around Sumar.

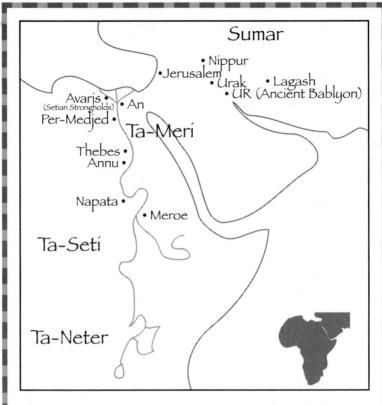

1900 BCE - Nipper is invaded by the mountain dwellers. As the holy city of the Anu federation in the Fertile Crescent, Nipper is where the High priesthood was centered. The 'Ibri' - Sumarian root of Ibrihim/Abraham - flee to An (Heliopolis) in the Nile Valley. Unite with the priesthood of Ra. They carry with them sacred stones that whisper and deposit them for safety in the Nile Valley. This is the biblical Abraham seeking refuge in Kemet from the famine. The Ibri are given the best of land - Tell Al Yahuda - The Mound of the Judah, near An. The Ibri reside in Kemet through the 14th dynasty (until around 1675 BCE).

1675 BCE - The Hyksos invade the Nile Valley. Hyksos are bands of desert shepherds who are organized by the Setian priesthood of

Ta-Seti to open a 2nd battlefront against the priesthood of Ra in Ta-Meri. The Setians attacked Ta-Meri from the South out of Nubia, and the Hyksos attacked Ta-Meri from the north out of Asia. The Hyksos overthrow the royal priest-kings of Ra and established the 15th-17th dynasties. 'There arose a Pharaoh who knew not Joseph'. The kings of these dynasties were Asian nomads propped up by the Setian priesthood. They oppressed the indigenous Nile Valley inhabits, enslaved them without mercy, and committed acts of genocide. The most wicked and ruthless was Apepa, who enslaved indigenous Kemites to build a temple to Set-Anup (the devouring jackal) and Apap (the Reptilians) at Het-uart (Avaris) in the Delta.

1555 BCE - Aahmose I (Yahmoses) overthrows Apepa and drives the Setians out of the Nile Valley. He reinstates the authority of the Amen-Ra Priesthood from Nubia to Palestine and begins the New Kingdom of the XVIII Dynasty. Yahmoses marries a princess from the Meroe/Napatan royal family to reunify the royal family of Ra and reestablish authority in Ta-Meri. This is the biblical Ethiopian bride, daughter of Jethro the High-Priest Magician. Yahmoses invades Palestine and what was ancient Sumar - the 'Promised Land' of the ancestral Ibri. Reclaims these territories from the Amorites and establishes sacred centers to Ra. Aahmose I is the biblical Moses who leads the nation of Israel (the children of Ra) out of bondage and into sacred land. Yahmose means 'Born of Yah'. Yah is the name of Ra as the lunar ark. Ra as the lunar ark comes as a deliverer of his children the Aahu (Iu), or those who "rise for Ra". Inscribed on the wall of An, the Auhu say "O impious cruel one Apap, who spreadest thy wickedness. Thy face shall be destroyed Apap! Approach thy place of torment… The Auhu are against thee: thou shalt be destroyed".

Yahmose is the biblical character who parts the waters to free the children (Aahu) of the most high of the Most High (Ra). As one who is born of the Lunar Ark of Ra, Yahmose is also builder of the Ark of the Covenant.

It is important to paint such a detailed portrait of Moses because his weapons of choice in his efforts to halt the incursions of the caucasian mountain dwellers were sacred stones. In fact, Moses is credited with creating two mythically powerful sacred stone tools - the Breastplates of the Levites and the Ark of the Covenant.

The Levites, the priestly order within the original nation, governed the sacred stone science. The Levites were 'Serpent Priests,' and the root of their name - Levi - means serpent, as is found in 'Leviathan' the sea serpent of the Bible. This is another affirming fact that the nation of Israel was actually the children of the Amon-Ra priesthood. The Biblical Serpent Priests of Levi corresponds to the Uraeaus crowns and headdress worn by the Ra priesthood in ancient Egypt. The uraeus embodies several things: protection of the mind's psychic potential, a raised kundalini (the serpentine fire of the central nervous system), and oneness with Ra.

The Sun disk of Ra is usually depicted with a cobra coiled beneath it. Thus, the cobra acts as a seat or throne upon which the soul of the Sun sits. Therefore, the cobra as a symbol was reserved for the priests, and kings of Ra - the Soul of the Sun. Legend states that the serpent Edjo protected Heru after his birth by the command of Ra. Thereafter, he protected each successive Pharaoh, whom was considered the living embodiment of Heru. To symbolize the protection of Edjo, each Pharaoh of Ra wears a Uraeus upon his crown. The Priests of *An*, being priests of Ra, wore the Uraeus upon their headdress. Surely, it is this priesthood that is the Serpent Priest of the Old Testament.

These Serpent Priests of the Bible worked with an amazing sacred stone science. Levite High Priest wore a Breastplate called an *Essen*. Upon the *Essen* were laid out twelve sacred stones in four rows of three: Sardius, Topaz, Carbuncle, Emerald, Sapphire, Diamond, Ligure, Agate, Amethyst, Beryl, Onyx and Jasper. The stones were connected in a circuitry of gold wire. On the reverse side of the *Essen* rested two mysterious stones (probably meteorites) called the *Urrim and Thummin* (Exodus, Chap. 39).

According to Flavius Josephus, the *Essen, Urrim, and Thummin* were used as a divination system. The *Urrim and Thummin* were thrown like dice, and how they rolled and landed was a means of revelation. Also, when a High Priest had the *Essen* on, he could ask Amen certain questions and the Spirit would respond through lighting up certain stones on the *Essen*. Josephus said that the last Breastplate stopped lighting up about 200 years before his life because the covenant had been broken.

The Levites also wore an *Ephod* - a vest with two shoulder buttons of onyx. It is reported that the onyx buttons would light up as a system of divination as well. When the right one lit up, it meant 'yes,' when the left shoulder button lit up, it meant 'no.'

This priestly attire also acted as protective gear; for it was the Levitical order who was responsible for the care of the Ark of the Covenant. The Ark is depicted in the Old Testament as a 'sanctuary' where the Great Spirit may dwell with hue-manity. Care for the Ark was a dangerous job that required a clean hand, a pure heart, and an ever-vigilant mind. There are several instances in the Old Testament of someone who was either not qualified or not righteous enough to be in the presence of the Ark. Bolts of energy would leap out from the Ark and destroy them instantly (Samuel, Chap. 4-6; Leviticus, Chap. 10; Numbers, Chap. 16).

In terms of modern technology, the Ark would be considered a leyden jar. A leydon jar is a specially designed capacitor that can store and emit powerful electrical charges. A capacitor is the technical name for a battery. A capacitor is constructed by placing an insulating material, usually wood or glass, between two conductive materials, usually metal. The Old Testament describes the Ark as being made of acacia wood that was inlaid inside and out with pure gold. [32]

Leyden jars are large vessels constructed as described. They are not like conventional batteries that can hold a charge after several discharges (uses). Leyden jars discharge their entire accumulation of energy at one time, and have to recharge to a certain capacity before they are able to discharge again.

Contrary to the popular view, the contents of the Ark are not the tablets of the Ten Commandments. The contents of the Ark are two highly energized meteorites. [33] The Nation of Israel, like most nations of her cultural milieu, organized herself around *Bet-Els*, sacred meteors from Heaven. Bet means 'House,' *El* means 'Celestial God-Force'. This indicates that in Hebrew, *Bet-Els* are considered the House of the heavenly father.

A modern example may be seen in Islam, which is organized around the Ka' aba. According to the Prophet Mohammed, The Black Stone of the Ka' aba fell from Heaven to Earth and was given to Adam to absorb his sins after the expulsion from the garden. In time, the Archangel Gabriel gave it to Ibrihim as a covenant stone. Later, Gabriel gave it to Mohammed, who made it the corner stone of the Ka' aba - 'Beating Heart' - of the Islamic world.

The Ark of the Covenant is the portable "Beating Heart" of Israel. Again, it is a very powerful electromagnetic capacitor. Upon the Ark rests "The Mercy Seat" where two winged cherubim sit with the *Shekinah*. The *Shekinah* is "The Celestial fire that burns the wicked". The Shekinah force manifests as a spark yielding 'pillar of cloud' which is generated by the *Bet-El's* energy discharging from the Ark.

The Kemetic origin of portable shrines is unquestionable. In fact, the two most important public ceremonies in Kemetic society were the enthroning of Pharaoh, and the procession of shrines. Wilkinson (1853), in *The Ancient Egyptians, Their Life and Customs, says:*

> One of the most important ceremonies was "the procession of the Shrines" which is mentioned in the Rosetta Stone, and is frequently represented on the walls of the temples. The shrines were of two kinds: the one a sort of canopy; the other an ark or sacred boat, which may be termed the great shrine. This was carried with grand pomp by the priests, a certain number being selected for that duty, who supporting it on their shoulders by means of long staves, passing through metal rings at the side of the sledge on which it stood, brought it into the temple, where it was placed upon a stand or table, in order that the prescribed ceremonies might be performed before it.... [34]

Wilkinson affirms that Kemetic Arks were often "overshadowed by the wings of two figures of the goddess Thmei or Truth, which call to mind the cherubim of the Jews".

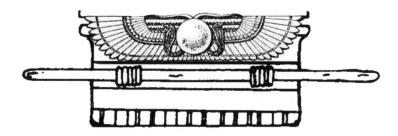

Moses is credited with creating the Ark, as well as designing the *Essen and Ephod*. Moses is also credited with being "learned in all the ways of the Egyptians." Certainly, Moses mastered this science while living in the Nile Valley; and Israel's sacred stone science may be seen as Kemet's stone science.

King Solomon is another Israelite fabled to have utilized powerful sacred stone sciences. Solomon was also most likely a Priest-King of the Amon-Ra Priesthood. According to the Old Testament, Solomon married the daughter of Pharaoh, and had relations with the Queen of Sheba (Kush). Therefore, it is doubtful that he was merely a vassal king of a small coastal city-state.

Solomon has been associated with the last two pharaohs of the XXI Dynasty - either Psusennes II or Siamun-meramun. The XXI dynasty has two historical periods - Rulership by The High Priests of Amen-Ra, and Rulership by the Kings of Tanis. Initially, the High Priests of Amon-Ra shunned giving absolute authority to one man as a way to avoid tyranny and despotism. However, there appears to have been a need to centralize power within the priesthood to maintain consistent governance of Kemet. The Kings of Tanis thus were Priests of Amon-Ra, but they ruled as Kings.

In this light, the Judges of the Old Testament - the counsel who ruled from Moses to Saul - are more than likely the High Priest of Amon-Ra who ruled from the XVIII dynasty through the first half of the XXI dynasty. Saul was the first Tanite King, and Solomon one of the most significant.

In the Talmud, there is a legend that the eight Heavenly Host descended from the celestial realm and presented Solomon with four jewels. Each jewel had a divine name inscribed on it, and each one gave Solomon dominion over a certain aspect of creation. One stone gave him dominion over the Heavenly Host; another dominion over the animal kingdom; another dominion over the terrain of the planet (the ability to create mountains, rivers, lakes, etc.); and the last dominion over the spirit kingdom - both positive and nefarious spirits.

Solomon had the four stones set in a signet ring so that he could sway rule over creation at any moment. Solomon then became obsessed with something contrary to an important Mosaic law - building a temple to house the Ark of the Covenant. Moses had commanded that the Ark never be housed indoors, but maintained by the Levites in groves of sacred trees. However, Solomon wanted to erect a temple "with a profusion of gold, silver, and precious stones, the like of which no ruler had ever possessed before him."

He commissioned Hiram Abiff of Tyre to erect the Temple, but when he heard the clamor created by the chisel and hammer upon the stones, he ordered that the temple be completed without the sound of chisel or hammer. He was told that the King of the nefarious jinn known as the Shedds could lead him to the Shamir stone - a "worm" stone that could cut any other stone with accurate precision by simply placing it on the desired area to be cut. The stone to be cut would magically and silently separate. The Shamir stone is legended to have been used by Aaron to cut the stones for the original Levitical Breastplates.

The King of the Shedds name is Ashmedai. Solomon ordered him bound by a gold chain with the divine name of Jah inscribed upon it and brought to him. Solomon then compelled Ashmedai to reveal the location of the Shamir. Ashmedai said the stone was in the belly of a wild rooster. Solomon quickly summoned the wild rooster and had him vomit up the Shamir stone. He then entrusted it to Hiram Abiff so that he and his master masons could complete the temple without the sound of a hammer. [35]

The temple of Solomon was specifically designed to recreate an image of heaven. The fact that he used a profusion of precious stones indicates that he considered sacred stones as embodying heavenly or celestial affinity. More than likely, Solomon probably considered heaven to appear as a realm made of sacred stones.

This is how heaven is depicted in Revelations of the New Testament, suggesting that this perspective of heaven passed from Judaic tradition to Christian tradition.

Chapter Four, entitled 'Around God's Throne' describes Iyahsus' ascent into Heaven. Iyahsus says of Heaven:

.... Behold, a throne was set in heaven, and behold one sat on the throne.

And he that sat on the throne was to look upon like jasper and a sardine stone: and there was a rainbow round about the throne, in sight like unto an emerald.

And round about the throne were four and twenty seats: and upon the seats I saw four and twenty elders sitting, clothed in white raiment; and they had on their heads crown of gold.... And before the throne there was a sea of glass like unto crystal....

This is another cultural manifestation that affirms that sacred stones are considered to be the Earthly home and throne of the One Most High (OMH) - The One God Creator. Moreover, considering that the throne of Most High is depicted as being in a sea of crystal, it may not be coincidental that *crystal* and *Christ* have a similar word-sound.

Contemporary Ethiopia

Contemporary Ethiopia must be surveyed at this point; for it is a living cultural embodiment of ancient Kush, Kemet, and Israel. As a result of Ethiopia's heritage, many of the sacred stone sciences used in ancient Kush, Kemet, and Israel survive in contemporary Ethiopia today. For example, five of Ethiopia's emperors have been mummified and preserved in the tradition of Kemetic pharaohs. The papyrus reed boats of pharaonic Egypt may be seen on Lake Tana in Ethiopia today. The tradition of creating Tekhets - obelisks - passed from the Northern Nile Valley into the Ethiopian highlands of Axum.

Another important cultural tradition that is preserved in Ethiopia today is the Ethiopian Orthodox Church's custodianship of the Biblical Ark of the Covenant. The Coptic Church of Ethiopia is the acknowledged caretaker of the Biblical relic, and claim that the Ark has been in Ethiopia since the time of Solomon.

As stated before, the Ark is a battery - a chamber made of an insulating material and coated inside and out with a conductive material. It is made of acacia wood (an insulator), and laid inside and out with gold (a conductor). As a battery, the ark can accumulate, store, and discharge great quantities of energy. Arks were a very important component of Kemetic spiritual ceremonies and temple processions. Moreover, what distinguished the biblical Ark from other Kemetic Ark shrines are its contents - two highly energized meteorites.

The legend of the arrival of the Ark is contained in the Ethiopian manuscript *The Kebra Negast*. It states that the Queen of Sheba was an Ethiopian named Makada, and that an Ethiopian merchant by the name of Tamrin (Amharic for Hiram) told her of a very wise man who lived in the north named Solomon.

Makada was eager to hear his wise mind in person, so she assembled a great caravan of gold, silver, precious stones, frankincense and myrrh. Makada traveled down the Nile with Tamrin, whereupon she presented Solomon with the wealth of Africa. However, Solomon coveted her pleasure more than her treasure. He swooned her with wise words, extolling good will, love and unity towards humanity. The Queen was impressed.

Solomon then pressed for some intimate love from the Queen. Makada explained that it is the custom of her nation that only a Queen may rule, and that she must remain virgin during her reign. Even though Solomon had 365 wives, he was mesmerized by the beauty of Makada and refused to accept no for an answer.

Solomon used his wise mind to create a deceptive plan. He asked Makada to have a feast with him, to which she agreed. He then asked the cook to prepare the food with an abundance of oils and spices. During the feast, Solomon asked Makada to rest in his chamber that evening. Makada was hesitant, but agreed on the condition that Solomon promise not to take her most precious treasure by force.

Solomon promised not to take her virginity if she did not take anything precious from him without first asking. Makada quickly agreed, knowing that her wealth was truly abundant. She naively could not conceive of needing anything precious from Solomon.

That night, Solomon had the chambermaid fill a bowl with water and place it in the room. He turned out the light and feigned sleep. Makada laid down in her bed, but could not sleep. The oily and spicy food made her restless and parched. She saw the bowl of water in the room and helped herself to a glass. At that point, Solomon jumped out of his bed and accused Makada of breaking her promise. Makada protested, saying that she was simply drinking a glass of water. At which point Solomon says", "Is there anything that thou hast seen under the heavens that is better than water?"

Makada reluctantly freed Solomon from his oath and he made love to her. That night, he had a frightening dream. The Sun was shining bright over Judah. Suddenly, it fell below the horizon and Judah was in darkness. The Sun then rose up in the Southern sky and shined on Ethiopia - the land to the South. However, Judah remained in darkness. Solomon awoke terrified. The dream disturbed Solomon so much; he did not share it with his High Priest Zadok, which was his usual custom.

The next day, Makada prepared herself to return to her country. Solomon prepared a massive caravan to ensure a safe, comfortable journey for the Queen. He also presented Makada with a ring, and asked her to use this as a sign if by chance she may have conceived from their union.

Makada returned to Ethiopia, and she did indeed conceive from their union. She bore a son, whom she named Menylek, "The Son of a Wise Man". On his eighteenth birthday, she presented Menylek with the ring Solomon gave her and asked Tamrin to guide Menylek to his father's land.

Menylek amazed the people of Judah, for his countenance was just like Solomon's. Solomon rejoiced upon meeting and coming to know Menylek, for his two other sons - Jeraboam and Rehaboam - were poor examples of men who incarnated Solomon's lustful and greedy tendencies. Solomon shared his entire wise mind with Menylek, and taught him in the ways of justice and righteous rulership. Menylek matured into a truly majestic prince.

As time progressed, Menylek decided to return home to Ethiopia. Solomon pleaded for him to stay and be king of Judah. Menylek refused. Solomon therefore decided that Menylek should establish a theocratic dynasty of Judaic kings in Ethiopia. To assist Menylek in this effort, Solomon instructed his priests to send their first-born sons with Menylek. Once in Ethiopia, the sons of the priests were to replicate the theocratic government of Judah.

Solomon's High Priest was named Zadok. He was Solomon's premier counselor and dream interpreter. Zadok was also the custodian of the Ark of the Covenant. The office of High Priest was inherited; therefore, the next person in line for custodianship of the Ark was Zadok's son Azaryus.

Azaryus spent his entire life dreaming of the day that he would be the custodian of the Ark. When Zadok informed him that he would be traveling to Ethiopia to be the High Priest for Solomon's son Menylek, Azaryus was devastated. That night, an angel appeared before Azaryus and told him of a plan to take the Ark.

He told Azaryus to make a wooden replica of the Ark and substitute it under the three covers that were usually kept over 'The Lady of Zion'. He did so and brought the Ark with him on his journey to Ethiopia. The Ark actually made the travel swifter and easier; the weather was as if God wanted them to arrive quickly and safely.

Solomon did not fare so well. When Menylek and the Sons of Judah departed, he shared his dream with Zadok of that fateful night. Zadok was struck with fear, for he interpreted the Sun in the dream to be the Ark. He quickly ran into the Holy of Holies and threw back the covers to reveal the wooden replica of the Ark. Zadok was so surprised, he collapsed and died on the spot.

Missing the Ark and his High Priest, Solomon rallied an army to pursue Menylek and Azaryus. However, they were met with foul weather, delays, and setbacks the entire journey. They turned back to Judah while still in the lower Nile region.

Coupled with this legend is a detailed description of the Ark in the *Kebra Negast*, which suggests that it is indeed in possession of the Ethiopian priesthood. It is contained in Chapter 17, entitled *'Concerning the Glory of Zion'*.

> And as concerning Zion, the Tabernacle of the Law of God: at the very beginning, as soon as God had established the heavens, He ordained that it should become the habitation of his glory upon the earth. And willing this He brought it down to the earth, and permitted Moses to make a likeness of it. And He said unto him, "Make an ark of wood that cannot be eaten by worms, and overlay it with pure gold. And thou shalt place therein the Word of the Law, which is the covenant that I have written with mine own fingers, that they may keep my law, the Two Tables of the Covenant." Now the heavenly and spiritual original within it is of divers colors, and the work thereof is marvelous, and it resembleth jasper, and the sparkling stone, and the topaz, and the hyacinthine stone, and the crystal, and the light, and it catcheth the eye by force, and it astonisheth the mind and stupefieth it with wonder, it was made by the mind of God and not by the hand of the Artificer, man, but He Himself created it for the habitation of His Glory. And it is a spiritual thing and is full of compassion; it is a heavenly thing and is full of light; it is a thing of freedom and a habitation of the Godhead, Whose habitation is in heaven, and Whose place of movement is on the earth, and it dwelleth with men

and with angels, a city of salvation for men and for the Holy Spirit a habitation. And within it are a Gomor of gold containing a measure of the manna which came down from heaven; and the rod of Aaron which sprouted after it had become withered though no one watered it with water, and it had broken it in two places, and it became three rods being originally only one rod... [36]

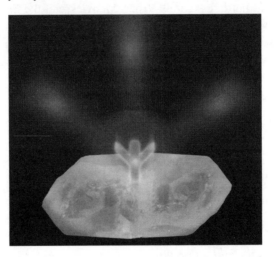

From this chapter, it can be gleaned that the Ark created by Moses was designed to be in the likeness of its contents, which is referred to as "The Word of the Law". The inner Ark is depicted as a symmetrical and multi-faceted gemstone that reflects many (divers) brilliant colors. It simultaneously appears like many different stones - jasper (ruddy red), the sparkling stone (maybe a highly translucent stone like diamond or Selenite), topaz (golden yellow) hyacinthine (associated with azure blue sapphire), and crystal (clear and translucent quartz).

Moreover, it is described as having a Gomor of gold. Gomer in the Old Testament means 'completion', or 'perfection'. Gomer has also been associated with 'bowl' or 'vessel'. Perhaps a gomer of gold refers to a symmetrical, crystalline gold inclusion.

The gold inclusion is also said to contain some 'manna'. Manna means 'what is it?', or the 'mystery that fell from the sky'. The manna may refer to a mineral that is not native to planet Earth and not identifiable within the table of elements. This earned the mysterious substance from space a name meaning 'What is it?' According to the Bible, this strange mineral that fell from the sky was a source of nutrition for the Nation of Israel during the 40-year sojourn in the wilderness.

Rising up from the gold is 'The Rod of Aaron', probably referring to an inclusion of iron. It is said to sprout from the gold and project through the stone. It splits into three rods that stick up out of the stone, the central one being shorter or 'withered'.

The inner Ark is said to be a heavenly thing, affirming that it was a bet-el (betyl or baetyl) or a meteorite. Moreover, it is either brilliantly translucent (reflects a lot of light) or photo-luminescent (emits its own light).

The passage states that Moses crafted the outer Ark to be in the likeness of the inner Ark. If this is so, the gold inlaid chest is in the likeness of the luminous stone matrix. The wings adorning the outer ark are in the likeness of the protruding Rods of Aaron. (Refer to back cover for color illustration of inner ark.)

The Priests of the Ethiopian Orthodox Church maintain that the glorious powers of the Ark remain, and that the Ark's energy has been used throughout Ethiopian history. The Guardian Priest of the Saint Mary of Zion Chapel in Axum, Berhane Meskel Zelelew says that the Ark was used to uplift the monolithic obelisks of Axum. These monuments are made of one stone, the most massive being one hundred ten feet tall and weighing five hundred tons. Moreover, Zelelew says that the Ark attracts the 'Celestial Fire', which is the actual power that uplifted the obelisks, acknowledging that no man could lift such massive objects. [37]

The Priests of the Ethiopian Orthodox Church also maintain that they have used the Ark several times in their role as Defender of the Faith. The Arch priest of the Saint Mary of Zion Ethiopian Orthodox Church in the United Kingdom, Solomon Gabre Selassie, says that in times of war, the priests have led the Ark out in Procession against the enemies. According to Selassie, the Ark was a:

> 'source of spiritual strength against the aggressors... The King would rally the people for battle and the priests would stand as on the day when

Joshua carried the Ark around the city of Jerico. Likewise our priests carried the Ark, chanting and going into battle in the glory of God'. [38]

The last time that the Ark was used in battle was near the turn of the century when Emperor Menylek II of Ethiopia used the Ark to defeat the Italians in the Battle of Adowa in 1896. The Italians were attempting to colonize Ethiopia, and had already subdued what is today Eritrea. The Italians were utilizing the latest in war technology, and had dispatched well equipped and numerous attack forces.

Menylek II rallied his provincial armies together. His troops were inexperienced in modern warfare, and their military weaponry was antiquated compared to the Italian troops. However, the Ethiopians delivered the Italians a devastating defeat, crushing the invading forces within six hours. It is generally acknowledged that the Ark was used in the battle and that it was the difference in the battle for the Ethiopians.

Without question, the Ark of the Covenant is the most significant expression of African sacred stone science within Ethiopia today. However, it is not the only way the Tawahedo Church utilizes sacred stones. In fact, stones are more often than not the focal point of communion with the 'Kristos' spirit.

For example, most churches are of Solomonic design. In other words, they have three concentric chambers. The outermost chamber is called *K'ene mahlet*, or the place where hymns are sung. The next chamber is the *K'eddest*, where communion is administered by priests to the congregation. The innermost chamber is called *mak'das*, or the 'Holy of Holies'. This place is also called *enda ta'amer*, or 'the place of miracle'. Only priests are allowed to enter the *mak'das*. At some churches, only a High Priest may enter. Inside the Holy of Holies are kept the Tabot (the Ark or a replica of it), and *Imre Bired* (the most sacred of stones).

An image of the *Imre Bired* within a *mak'das* is contained within the *Kebra Negast*.

And God commanded Moses and Aaron to make holy vessels for the Tabernacle of Testimony for the furnishing of the holy of Holies, namely vessels of gold, bowls and pots, pitchers and sacred tables, netted cloths and tops for pillars, lamps and vessels for filling them, torchholders and snuffers, tongs, candlesticks, and rings and rods for carrying them, large bowls and lavers, embroidered curtains and hangings, crowns and worked vestments, purple cloths and leather work, carpets and draperies, unguents for anointing priests and kings, hyacinthine and purple hangings, rugs of double thickness and hangings of silk, skins of kids and red hides of rams, and *Sardius stones, and rubies, and sapphires, and emeralds* - to place them in the Tabernacle of Witness, where dwelleth Zion, the habitation of His Glory....[39]

The *mak'das*, or Holy of Holies is considered the dwelling place of God, and the congregation comes within the *k'eddest* to commune with the Holy Spirit that is in the mak'das. This is yet another African cultural manifestation that affirms that:

- Sacred stones are central tools in the spiritual expression, religious rites and rituals of African cultures.

- Sacred stones are considered the Earthly home and throne of the One Most High (OMH) - The One God Creator. As such, they are also vehicles through which communion may occur.

There are even greater and more complex expressions of these themes within the Tawahedo Church. As previously stated, Ethiopia is the oldest Judeo-Christian nation extant today. The Solomonic Dynasty of Kings has ruled in Ethiopia since it was founded around 960 BCE by Menylek I, son of Solomon and Sheba. There have been 225 Kings in this lineage, the last one being Emperor Haile Selassie I who ruled through 1976. This lineage has been interrupted only one time in this 2800-year period. That was from the mid 1100's - 1270 BCE when the Zagwe Dynasty of Kings assumed the throne of Ethiopia and was formally recognized by the Tawahedo Church as the legitimate seat of power.

The Zagwe came to power when a strong warrior Queen named Gudit (Judith) unified clans of Bet Israel (Falasha) and Islamic clans and overran Aksum. Once they were recognized as the sovereign rulers of the kingdom, they moved the capital from Axum north to Roha.

The Zagwe speak an Agau language, which is considered to be in the Kushitic language family. Kushitic languages are also known as Nilolitic languages, or languages indigenous to the Nile Valley regions. They are distinct from Semitic languages, the origins of this language family being Asia. The Zagwe have been in the horn of Africa for a very long time, and are the original indigenous people of the regions of Aksum, Tigrai, Begemder (source of Blue Nile), Angot, and Shoa.

As can be gleaned from the story of Queen Gudit, the Zagwe have a strong Judeo-Christian heritage. According to their traditions, the Zagwe are descendants of Moses and his Kushite wife. As a result, the Zagwe practiced Judaism (lived Mosaic Law) from around the time Biblical Israel was founded as a nation - probably around 1450 BCE.

In time, many Zagwe blended the Kristos tradition ('Kristos' is the Ethiopian form of Christian) into their Judaic heritage. By the mid 1100's, many Zagwean royalty became *Debtera* (educated chanters and scholars) within the Tawahedo Church. Five Zagwe actually assumed the throne as Priest-King:

- Marari
- Yimrha Kristos
- Lalibala
- Na'akueto la'ab
- Yetbarak Za'elmaknum

These Zagwe Kings, particularly Yimrha Kristos and Lalibala, sponsored many Church expansions; and are responsible for the incredible 'Churches of Living Rock' of Roha. Yimrha Kristos built the first 'Church of the Living Rock'. Lalibala then had 11 more built in an effort to create a "New Jerusalem" at Roha.

The chronicle of Lalibela's life is fascinating. At the moment of his birth, he was swarmed by a mass of bees. This earned him the name "the Bees honor his sovereignty". During his ascension to the throne, it is said that angels came and took Lalibela into the First, Second, and Third Heavens. While in these regions, Lalibela was given instructions to create a 'New Jerusalem' at Roha. He was to construct 11 Rock Hewn Churches. The Angels were going to assist in his efforts.

Once he returned to Earth, Lalibela carried out his instructions. He assembled a group of masons, carpenters, and craftsman. The angels joined the masons in the day and worked with them in carving the churches. At night, the angels worked alone and completed twice as much work when uninterrupted by their human partners. In 24 years, all 11 rock-hewn churches were complete.

Rock Hewn Churches are carved out of mountains or into the earth. Shaped like equilateral crosses, the Churches act as a sacred geometric chamber connected to the life force of planet Earth. Moreover, these churches are also built upon Solomonic design, and contain within their center a Holy of Holies chamber fitted with Imre Bired.

The implication of a Church designed in such a fashion is that the Earthly Home and Throne of the Kristos Spirit is considered to be within sacred stones. The intention of carving the church out of living rock still connected to the planet may be to send healing and purifying energy into the earth. It may also be designed to augment, increase, and amplify the energy within the Holy of Holies (mak'das).

There is an Ethiopian Church manuscript entitled *The Book of Enoch*, that gives insight into the experience one might have inside a mak'das. Enoch is one of the great Patriarchs within the Biblical Genesis. He is credited with being the only Patriarch to ascend to heaven and return to Earth, as well as the one Patriarch who ascended into Heaven while still in the flesh instead of dying a mortal passing. The story of Enoch's travels in the heavens is very similar to Lalibela's ascension story. When Enoch traveled the heavens, he was taught the sciences of reading, writing, astronomy, and agriculture. Once he returned to Earth, he is credited with teaching these sciences to humanity.

The Book of Enoch is an ancient text, fragments of which have been found in Middle Eastern languages of Greek, Latin, and Aramaic. However, the complete Book has been found only in Ge'ez - the liturgical language of the Tawahedo Church.

In the Book, Enoch recounts two stone visions that he experienced. The first one involves Enoch ascending into heaven and entering the crystal palace of 'The Ancient of Days'.

> A vision thus appeared to me. Behold, in that vision clouds and a mist invited me; agitated stars and flashes of lightening impelled and pressed me forward, while winds in the vision assisted my flight, accelerating my progress. They elevated me aloft to heaven. I proceeded, until I arrived at a wall built with stones of crystal. A vibrating flame of fire surrounded it, which began to strike me with terror. Into this vibrating flame I entered; And drew nigh to a spacious habitation built also with stones of crystal. Its walls too, as well as pavement, were formed with stones of crystal. and crystal likewise was the ground. Its roof had the appearance of agitated stars and flashes of lightening; and among them were cherubim of fire in a stormy sky. A flame burned around its walls; and its portal blazed with fire. When I entered into this dwelling, it was hot as fire and cold as ice... [39]

Once in the crystal palace, the Ancient of Days reveals to Enoch the fate of the righteous and wicked on planet earth, as well as the cycles and order of the celestial realm. He orders Enoch to return to Earth and write these things down as the revealed Word for Hue-manity.

The second stone vision involves Enoch traveling 'The Path of the Angels':

> I perceived at the extremity of the earth the firmament of heaven above it. Then I passed on towards the south; where burnt, both day and night, six mountains formed of glorious stones; three towards the east, and three towards the south. Those which were towards the east were of a variegated stone; one of which was of margarite, and another of antimony. Those towards the south were of a red stone. The middle one reached to heaven like the throne of God; a throne composed of alabaster, the top of which was of sapphire. I saw too, a blazing fire hanging over all the mountains. And there I saw a place on the other side of an extended territory, where waters were collected. I likewise beheld terrestrial fountains, deep in the fiery columns of heaven... [40]

Perhaps the *Imre Bired* within the *Mak'das* is designed to allow the High Priest to travel to the Crystal Palace of the 'Ancient of Days' and glorious stone mountains of 'The Path of the Angels'.

Without a doubt, sacred stones are central tools in the spiritual expression and religious rituals of Ethiopia. In fact, it can be said that all six themes outlined at the beginning of the chapter are extant today within the Kristos Tradition:

- The Ethiopians synergistically blended their melanin with sacred stones through the adorning of self with crowns, jewelry, etc.

- Sacred stones are central tools in the spiritual expression and religious rites of the Tawahedo Church.

- Sacred stones are considered vehicles through which communion with The One God Creator can occur.

- Clear Quartz Crystal is considered to be the Earthly home and throne of the One Most High (OMH) - The One God Creator.

- Meteorites, or Bet-Els are considered to be covenant stones, or stones through which the guidance and protection of the Most High God (OMH) is made manifest. This is exemplified in the Tawahedo Church claim to be in custody of the Ark of the Covenant.

The Originals Of Australia

The Originals (disrespectfully called aboriginal) of Australia call themselves the Arunta. Their ancestors migrated out of ancient Kush/Kemet approximately 50,000 years ago. They brought their sacred stone science with them and preserved it well within their Pacific Island habitat. Their perspective and application of crystal science is fascinating.

These humans, like their Ethiopian brethren, view God's Home, Throne, and Spirit as being localized on earth within crystal. This perspective of crystals as divine stones is the central science within the initiation and rites of passage of the Australian Originals. Their system of initiation is actually a process of deification of the neophyte: transforming a man-child into a man-god.

James Cowan, author of *Mysteries of the Dream Time*, surveys Australian Original culture and points out the following sacred stone applications:

- An East Coast group reveres clear quartz, which they call 'wild stones.' They say the stones embody the 'Great Spirit' himself.

- Other Originals, including the Dayaks, say that quartz has celestial origins, that the throne of Biaimi - The Great Creator - is made of crystal. These stones fell to Earth as 'solidified light.'

- During the initiation rites of the Central Australian Arunta, the Karadji (neophyte) experiences a ritual in which priests would pull crystals out of their own bodies and press them into the neophyte at certain points. The skin would be cut at times and crystals would be implanted in the incision. More stones would be inserted into the scalp, the tongue, and the first finger of the right hand later in the rite. It culminates with the Karadji eating food and drinking water into which small amounts of crushed crystals had been placed.

- Another nation has a similar initiation process, but they actually remove internal organs of the Karadji and replace them with a new set and quartz crystal.

These rites are designed to transform the neophyte into a man-god by creating a powerful light-body which overflows with a magic force called *gedji*. The ultimate source of the gedji is the clear quartz, which they call *'gedji stones.'* With these inside their body, the deified *'Oruncha'* can do magic, heal, see vast distances and into other realms. They can commune with the ancestors and "see into the underworld."

The similarities between the initiation rites of the Kemites and the Arunta are striking. As outlined previously, the central focus of the Kemetic initiation process is implanting and laying on the body sacred stones in ritualistic ceremonies. Here this initiation practice has been preserved for thousands of years in the South East Pacific.

The Dogon Of Mali

The Dogon of West Africa dwell in a mountainous terrain near the border of Mali and Upper Volta. The Dogon have been the center of many debates, for they have knowledge of the Sirius Star system that western scientist was able to confirm only with using high powered telescopes. Some Dogon cosmological science was revealed through their interaction with two French anthropologists: Marcel Griaule and Germaine Dieterlen. Most of Griaule and Dieterlen's work has been translated into English in two books, *Conversations with Ogotemmeli* and *The Pale Fox.* [42]

Stones play a vital role in Dogon cosmology and high-science. According to Ogotemmeli, the Dogon are the ascendants of eight great celestial ancestors called *The Nommo*. The Nommo originate from *'Kora Na'* -The Pure Earth: A watery planet in the Sirius Star System. The Nommo are depicted as four pairs of androgynous, amphibious human twins. One of the Nommo - *Lebe* - was sacrificed and his blood and life force was sprinkled upon planet Earth to purify it from its sins. This planet, according to Ogotemmeli, is an impure Earth created in inharmonious impurity by Ogo, *The Pale Fox*.

Lebe's spirit re-incarnated in the Hollow Earth (Underworld), and he united with the Earth to give birth to eight families of humans in the image of the eight celestial Nommo. The humans ascended to the surface of the planet with the mission to be fruitful, multiply, and balance the planet through prayer (*So Tanie* - The Astonishing Word) and agriculture. *Lebe* also sacrificed 8 of his bones to be covenant stones for the eight families. These bones are the *'Dague'* stones of the *Hogon*, the High Priest and Head Counsel for each family.

Ogotemmeli says that Lebe was sacrificed:

> "in order that men should believe that the stones were his bones digested and transformed... in order that the affair [of planetary salvation] should be an affair of men and not of heaven, so that something of heaven should become part of human nature; it was to make men believe that the aged Lebe, the oldest and most venerable of them all, and he alone, was present in the covenant-stones. It was so that men might understand all

the things he had done, that the Nommo came down on to the skeleton of a man..."

These meteoric Bet-Els give the Hogon incredible powers. He is the healer, diviner, defender of the community, and most importantly, the steward of the planet. As the custodian of the clan's covenant stone, his character must be upright. So, when it is time for a Hogon to be replaced because of age by another initiate, the Hogon will hide the Dague stone deep into the natural elements. The rightful custodian is then either guided to the Dague stone after much meditation, purification, and prayer. Or, the Hogon can win favor of a totem animal of his clan to go to the Dague stone. The animal will find the stone, swallow it, return to the Hogon, and vomit it up. Upon receiving the Dague stone, the Hogon then must establish and consecrate an altar to Lebe.

Other West African Nations

The Dogon are not the only West African clan who utilizes sacred stone science. Throughout West Africa, Hue-man's worked the sacred stone science in a similar fashion. Butt-Thompson (1969) in *'West African Secret Societies,'* has identified the following practices of West African High Priests: [43]

- Crystal gazing,' or 'Crystal vision' is common to most West African Secret Orders. It is a science usually reserved for the Head Priest. The stones are revered as sacred, are rarely brought outside the council house, and are carefully covered during thunderstorms because they often attract lightening.

- The Ngbe and the Nimm work intensely with amber in their rites.

- The Oro, Egbo, and Ogboni work with stones that nature has roughly shaped into human form. The Oro's is a Bet-El, which was passed from an ancestral migratory clan from the East.

- The Egbo High Priest has a Bet-El shaped like a five-pointed star. It is said to have fallen from Heaven to a part of Nigeria ages ago. It is kept oiled and covered in hide. The Bet-El's shape is the emblem of the society, and they decorate their staffs with metal pentagrams inset with ivory and crystal.

Summation: Sankofa

The Adinkra symbol Sankofa of the Akan is often translated *"One must look to the past before one may step to the future"*. This is the spirit in which *Stone Ages* is presented; for, the human/mineral connection has always manifested as *cultural greatness* and *spiritual unfoldment* for People of Color.

It is time to go back and claim this cultural heritage as the foundation of a strong spiritual technology for the new millennium.

Aya

Aya

Aya embodies **endurance, defiance against adversity, Self-determination, perseverance and resourcefulness.** *Aya* provides the principles by which melaninated people may empower themselves with sacred stones.

Aya explores how this ancient-yet-futuristic spiritual technology may be used to harmonize the external environment and inner-worlds of African people. *Aya* also explores how sacred stones may be used to heal our relationships and ourselves. *Aya* **reveals how one may use the Rocks of Ages to gain mastery of the vibrations within one's reality.**

Aya says that the eternal road may be rocky, but know that the stones we trod upon are the *Rocks of Ages.* Sacred stones are not stumbling blocks, they are stepping stones that elevate our awareness, increase our resourcefulness, and teach us to persevere. *Yes Aya!*

Aya

Aya - Spiritual Technologies for the New Millennium

Principles For Overstanding The Properties Of The Mineral Nation

One of the greatest gifts the mineral kingdom has to offer hue-manity is a strong intuition. Intuition is inner knowing: tapping the wealth of infinite knowledge available to our super-conscious mind. There is a saying attributed to the old folks: *Think long and you think wrong - Use your first mind.* This first mind is our super-conscious mind, that part of our awareness connected to the omniscient awareness of the universe. The omniscient awareness of the universe exists in all things within creation. It is 'common sense' - the awareness common to all. The stones speak to hue-manity, but hue-manity cannot hear with physical ears - the stones' voice is heard by the inner ears of the super-conscious mind.

Within the human mind is a constant stream of inner-communication. Think about it for a minute: We experience 'thought' as words spoken by our mind. Unfortunately for many people, inner-communication is an unconscious process and many do not discern the origins of the different thoughts they act out and experience. It is unfortunate because it often leads to self-doubt, poor decision making, as well as unnecessary disorder and chaos in one's life.

The process of learning about sacred stones should also be a process of self-discovery. Learning to communicate with the mineral nation should coincide with learning the nature of one's own inner-communication. Because of this, general principles by which one can comprehend the mineral kingdom are explored in this section. Specific or detailed directions for using the stones are avoided. *Aya* is devoted to empowering the readers to figure out for themselves the best way for utilizing any sacred stone. The act of figuring out for Self the specific applications of various stones leads to a stronger sense of inner-knowing / intuition.

I urge the reader to allow the stones to whisper into your inner ear as to how to specifically relate to them. The result will be a stronger mastery of mind, organized thoughts, and open channels of intuitive knowing. It will also make the reader's exploration of the mineral kingdom a unique and personally empowering experience.

Principle One

Identify the minerals that compose the stone. Then correspond the properties of the stone with the mineral's function within the body.

Minerals are chemical elements that are assimilated into the human body and are vital for a healthy life. Minerals that are needed in significant quantity daily are called essential minerals. Minerals that are needed in occasional small amounts are called trace minerals. The key minerals essential to life include (in alphabetical order): Calcium, Carbon, Chlorine, Chromium, Copper, Fluorine, Hydrogen*, Iron, Lithium, Magnesium, Manganese, Nitrogen*, Oxygen*, Phosphorus, Potassium, Selenium, Silicon, Sodium, Sulfur, and Zinc.

*Oxygen, Hydrogen, and Nitrogen are technically considered elements, not minerals. However, they are often contained in crystalline mineral structures.

Identify the minerals that compose the stone. Then correspond the properties of the stone with the mineral's function within the body. For example, the sacred stone calcite is composed of calcium, carbon and oxygen. Within the human body, calcium is the key mineral for proper development of the skeletal system. The skeletal system provides structure for the body. Therefore, through correspondence, it can be said that calcium aids in creating a healthy psycho-spiritual structure.

The calcium in calcite helps one create a firm structure of habits that would define a holistic, healthy lifestyle - just as the skeletal system creates the firm structure upon which a whole, complete body is built.

Carbon is the primary organizing mineral within the body. Carbon impacts on cell organization, blood sugar absorption (energy transfer), protoplasmic (intracellular fluid) function, and muscle metabolism. Through correspondence, it can be said that on a psycho-spiritual level, carbon empowers one to organize and balance how their life force energy is harnessed and made manifest.

Oxygen is the life-giving element in air, and is vital for the fire of life (spirit) to burn within the body. Through correspondence, it can be said that the oxygen in calcite would augment oxygen intake and absorption - increasing the flow of life force (spirit) within the body.

Synthesizing the properties of the three minerals, it can be said that calcite may promote a change in habits and lifestyles (one's psycho-spiritual structure). The change in habits more than likely would lead to an increase in the intake and assimilation of oxygen into the body (i.e. - quit smoking, initiate exercise routine, reconnect with natural environments, etc.). The result may be that the person connecting with the calcite is empowered to organize and balance how their life force energy is harnessed and made manifest.

A brief summary of the essentials and trace minerals role in the body, and stones containing the minerals is as follows.

Calcium:

An essential mineral, calcium is the primary building block for skeletal and dental structure. Calcium is necessary for proper fetal growth and formation. Soothes the nervous system.

Stones: Apatite, Apophyllite, Aragonite, Calcite, Danburite, Dolomite, Epidote, Flourite, Gypsum, Labradorite, Prehnite, and Zoisite.

Carbon:

An essential mineral that is the building block of organic matter. A complex molecular structure empowers carbon to be the foundation of amino acids, carbohydrates, glucose, and saccharides in the body. Carbon impacts on cell organization, sugar absorption (energy transfer), protoplasmic function, and muscle metabolism.

Stones: Aragonite, Calcite, Carbonite, Carbon Quartz, Smoky Quartz, Diamond, Magnesite, Malachite, Matrix of Herkimer Diamonds, Melanite, Rhodochrosite, and Smithsonite.

Chlorine:

An essential mineral, chlorine is a cleansing element, and aids in the expelling of waste and impurities from the body. It is also germicidal and anti-bacterial. It is a key element in the digestive process; and mixed with hydrogen forms hydrochloric acid, the necessary digestive secretion of the stomach. Chlorine also has analgesic (pain reducing) properties.

Stones: Apatite, Halite, Sodalite

Chromium:

A trace mineral, chromium is responsible for proper insulin/glucose balance in the blood and proper functioning of the spleen and pancreas.

Stones: Chromite

Copper:

Copper is a trace mineral which is present in all body tissues. It is a key element of the amino acid tyrosine, a major building block of melanin. Copper partners with iron in hemoglobin production, and is vital for the body to be able to conduct ionic energy.

Stones: Antlerite, Azurite, Boleite, Bornite, Chalcanthite, Chalcocite, Chalcopyrite, Chrysacolla, Copper, Covellite, Cuprite, Dioptase, Malachite, Tennantite, Tetrahedite, Turquoise

Fluorine:

Fluorine fortifies the body and reinforces all hard tissue within the body (bones, teeth, ligaments, sinus, nails, etc.). Fluorine acts as an anti-oxidant and prevents decay of these tissues. It also has germicidal and disinfecting qualities.

Stones: Cryolite, Flourite, Microlite

Hydrogen:

Hydrogen is probably the most 'essential' element there is. It means 'to produce water', and hydrogen is the moisturizing element of the body. All living organisms contain this most basic of elements. Water is the medium within which all cellular activity takes place, and hydrogen is present in most biochemical processes.

Stones: (Note that hydrogen is in many stones; the more common and/or powerful for spiritual technology are listed) Antigorite, Apatite, Apophyllite, Azurite, Childrenite, Chrysacolla, Dioptase, Epidote, Lazulite, Lepidolite, Malachite, Opal, Serpentine, Tourmaline, Turquoise, Zoisite.

Iron:

Iron is an essential mineral that is the foundation of healthy blood. It is iron that permits the blood to attract oxygen from the air drawn into the lungs and then carry it throughout the body. Anemia and general physical debility occurs without sufficient iron. An abundance of iron promotes vitality, courage, and radiance.

Stones: Almadine, Antigorite, Childrenite, Franklinite, Hematite, Limonite, Magnetite, Marcasite, Olivine, Pyrite, Tourmaline (black), Serpentine, Staurolite

Lithium:

As a trace mineral, lithium is necessary in minute amounts for mental stability. Lithium is very useful in treating depression and/or substance abuse of all kinds.

Stones: Elbaite, Lepidolite

Magnesium:

Magnesium is an essential mineral that is a relaxing and nourishing to the nervous system. It is vital for proper brain function, and promotes fruitful sleep. Magnesium alkalizes the body, cools and soothes fevers/inflammations, and sharpens perception.

Stones: Almandine, Antigorite, Augite, Hypersthene, Idocrase, Lazulite, Magnesite, Olivine, Pyrope, Serpentine, Talc

Manganese:

Manganese is an essential mineral that improves memory, perception, and coordinated thought and action. Manganese balances bile activity, harmonizes the nervous system, and increases resistance/immune response. It relieves impatience and anxiety, and increases the capacity for one to experience love and joy.

Stones: Childrenite, Chloritoid, Columbite, Helvite, Manganite, Pyrolusite, Rhodochrosite, Rhodonite, and Wolframite

Nitrogen:

Nitrogen is another key element found in organic chemistry. It is a base component of amino acids and melanin compounds. Nitrogen is found in the flesh, tissue, body fluids, hair, skin, nails, eyes and connective tissue. It is the element responsible for holding and binding the body and its parts together.

Stones: Niter

Oxygen:

Oxygen means 'to produce acid', meaning it is the volatile, active element in biochemistry. Oxygen is essential to health, and every cell needs a supply of it to be vital. The 'giver of life' helps with the assimilation of nutrients, promotes cell regeneration, strengthens mental acuity, and helps the body maintain a youthful vigor.

Stones: Agate, Albite, Antigorite, Apatite, Apophyllite, Aragonite, Azurite, Beryl, Calcite, Celestite, Childrenite, Chrysocolla, Corundum, Cuprite, Danburite, Dioptase, Franklinite, Hematite, Kyanite, Labradorite, Lazulite, Lazurite, Lepidolite, Limonite, Magnesite, Magnetite, Malachite, Olivine, Opal, Phenakite, Quartz, Rhodochrosite, Rhodonite, Rutile, Serpentine, Sodalite, Topaz, Tourmaline, Turquoise, Willemite, Zoisite

Phosphorus:

This element's name means 'The Light Bearer', which it earned because it has the ability to radiate light. Phosphorescence is what makes a firefly light up the night sky. Within the human body, phosphorus is the element the brain uses to think, memorize, visualize, and reason. Phosphorus is the medium through which the light of the soul can shine forth from the mind into the external world. Phosphorus improves sexual function and is vital for reproduction. It also is present in muscle tissue and bone structure.

Stones: Amblygonite, Apatite, Brazilianite, Childrenite, Lazulite, Monazite, Pyromorphite, and Turquoise

Potassium:

Potassium is an alkalizing element, and is vital for maintaining proper ph balance within the body. It neutralizes acidic conditions, alkalizes the blood, which in turn increases the efficiency of all of the body's systems. Potassium eliminates waste from cells, improves the body's healing powers, and prevents health challenges. It is vital for proper circulation and nerve functioning.

Stones: Adularia, Alunite, Apophyllite, Lepidolite, Leucite, Muscovite, Neptunite, Niter, Sanidine, and Sylvite

Selenium:

Selenium is a trace mineral that is needed for the body to maintain elasticity. Selenium allows the body to grow and mature properly, and is needed for fertility in both men and women.

Stones: Selenite

Silicon:

Silicon plays a vital role in the nervous system; it facilitates the transmission of neural impulses. It is considered a 'magnetic' element, and it provides the Electro-magnetic polarity needed for neural impulses to jump from neuron to neuron. Silicon is also a building block for hair, bone, teeth, skin, and nails. It allows these structures to maintain a firm-yet-elastic quality.

Stones: Agate, Antigorite, Apophyllite, Beryl, Chrysacolla, Danburite, Dioptase, Epidote, Kyanite, Labradorite, Lazurite, Lepidolite, Opal, Phenakite, Quartz, Serpentine, Sodalite, and Topaz

Sodium:

Sodium is another alkalizing element. It aids in keeping the lymphatic system and the blood alkalized. Sodium is stored in the stomach, and is the element that neutralizes stomach acids. It is essential to proper digestion. Liver, spleen, and pancreas function is dependent upon sodium. Sodium is also an electrolyte (ion carrier) within the body's fluids.

Stones: Albite, Ague, Brazilianite, Halite, Labradorite, Lazurite, Scapolite, Black Tourmaline, and Sodalite

Sulfur

Sulfur is a key element within melanin, being the basis of the amino acid cysteine. Sulfur is vital for regulating body temperature and the body's ability to produce and maintain heat. Sulphur detoxifies the body, stimulates fertility in men and women, gives hair, nails, and skin complexion a radiant glow, and balances the nervous system.

Stones: Cobaltite, Gypsum, Lazurite, Marcasite, Pyrite, and Sulfur

Zinc

Zinc is a trace element, but it is very important for the human body. DNA synthesis and replication is dependent upon sufficient zinc. As a result, zinc is key to health of the reproductive system, and plays a role in the healing of cuts, burns, and injuries. Approximately 25 enzymes that play a role in digestion and respiration contain zinc.

Stones: Zincite, Wurtzite, Willemite, Smithsonite, and Franklinite[1]

Principle Two:

Identify the origin of the stone, then relate the qualities. For example:

Meteorites, or stones that fall from space, usually connects one with the heavens and humanity's celestial origins. Tektites (silica-based meteorites) and space metals (iron and nickel-based meteorites) are examples.

River stones, or stones that have been smoothed and rounded by rushing water, tend to calm and purify feelings. These stones can be found in any running stream, creek, or river. Shiva linghams from the Narmada River in India are highly venerated river stones. These stones contain a meteoritic material, and are naturally rounded into a phallic or egg-like shape.

Ocean stones, or stones that come from the salt waters of the Earth, tend to invoke abundance and nurturing. The salt seas have been associated with the Great Mother by many cultures throughout the ages. These stones bring her presence and qualities. These stones are most commonly found at beaches.

Mountain stones, or stones that come from the high places of the Earth, tend to elevate consciousness. These stones take one to the heights, their home on Earth. Clear Quartz is often mined from mountain ranges.

Inner-Earth stones, or stones that are from deep within volcanic vents or the Earth's mantle, tend to take one within self. Obsidian, which is volcanic glass, or serpentine, which is derived from the earth's mantle, are examples of inner-earth stones. They assist one in getting their inner worlds in order.

Organic stones, or stones that were once a part of a living organism, tend to connect one with nature. Amber, seashells, fossils, petrified wood, and coral are examples of organic stones. They allow one to feel the life force in other beings.

Principle Three:

Identify how stone was formed, and then relate the qualities. For example:

Igneous stones are rocks that are formed by heat and pressure. Obsidian (volcanic glass) is an example. These stones help us withstand the pressure and challenges of life.

Metamorphic stones develop by changing their form because of environmental forces. Garnet, tourmalines, and Kyanite are examples of metamorphic rock. These stones help us change, grow, transform, and adapt.

Sedentary stones are stones that aggregate or grow because of weathering. Calcites, Sandstone, and stalagmites are examples of sedentary stones. These stones help us endure the cycles of time.

Principle Four:

Identify the Electro-magnetic potential within the stone. In other words, does the stone have:

- Piezoelectric potential (creates electricity from pressure) example: Quartz crystal

- Photoelectric potential (creates electricity from light) example: Selenite

- Pyroelectric potential (creates electricity from heat) example: Tourmaline

- Magnetic potential (emits a magnetic field and has magnetic attraction) example: Magnetite/lodestone

- Paramagnetic potential (emits magnetic field but does not have magnetic attraction) example: Pyrite

A stone's electro-magnetic potential determines the way it creates and / or discharges energy.[2]

Principle Five:

Identify the hardness of the stone, then relate it to its qualities.
Generally speaking, soft stones teach us to be delicate and tactful. They
smooth our rough edges. Hard stones teach us eternal truths and how to
endure throughout time.

The hardness is determined by looking up the stone on the Mohs
(pronounced Moe's) Hardness scale. Moh is a scientist who developed
a relative scale of stone hardness. He gave the softest stone he could
find (talc) the value of one. He then gave the hardest stone (diamond)
the value of 10. Based on this, each stone is ranked on the scale of 1-
10, depending on how hard the stone is.

*For example:

Mohs scale	Stone
1	Talc
2	Gypsum
3	Calcite
4	Flourite
5	Apatite
6	Turquoise
7	Quartz
8	Topaz
9	Corundum (Ruby & Sapphire)
10	Diamond [3]

Principle Six:

**Determine the translucence of the stone, or its ability to reflect and
refract light.**

Generally speaking, highly translucent stones such as clear quartz and
selenite teach us to be visionary, radiant, and reflective. Non-translucent

stones such as pyrite and bloodstone tend to effect the physical body, and are good for regenerating damaged organs, tissues, etc.

Principle Seven:

Consider all other physical features of the stone. They are obvious indicators as to how to best use the stone.

Some physical features to look for include:

Terminations - Do the ends of the stone come to a natural geometric point?

Striations - Are there a series of parallel lines running the length or width of the stone?

Size & Shape - Small stones tend to make excellent travel companions. Larger stones tend to create a harmonious atmosphere/environment in the home or business place.

Color - Each color has a different impact upon the mind and body. Color therapy with sacred stones is explored more in-depth in *bioresonance.*

Principle Eight:

Balance elevating stones with grounding stones.

Depending on the vibration a stone emits, it will have one of two effects on one's perspective or focus of awareness. The stone may cause one's focus to expand, elevate, travel, drift, and ascend into higher mental and spiritual planes; or it may ground, concentrate, center, and fix focus of awareness squarely in the material plane.

One must be aware to ground oneself when wearing elevating stones. Signs of not being grounded include:
- Excessive daydreaming, idealizing, and fantasizing;
- Lack of productivity, procrastination, poor work habits;
- Lack of financial resources;
- Forgetfulness, lack of concentration, disorganization;

- Headaches, head complaints, eye and vision challenges;
- 'Airheadedness'

One must be aware to balance grounding stones as well. Signs of being over-grounded include:

- Depression or melancholy;
- Feeling over-burdened and overly frustrated;
- Compulsive work habits;
- Inability to relax, unwind, and manage stress;
- Pre-occupation with materialism, consumerism, and working to acquire things.
- Lack of balance between material and spiritual values.

A spectrum of elevating and grounding stone are as follows:

Highly elevating stones: Phenakite, Moldavite tektites, Selenite, Optical clear calcite.

Elevating stones: Quartz crystal, Apophyllite, Celestite, Space metals (Gibeon), Amethyst, Kyanite, Azurite, Danburite, Elestial quartz, Apatite.

Neutral stones: Moonstone, Antigorite, Adventurine, Malachite, Chrysacolla, Rhodonite, Rhodochrosite, Silver, Copper, and Serpentine.

Grounding Stones: Carnelian, Moki marbles, Hematite, Pyrite, Franklinite, Green Tourmaline, Smoky Quartz, Agates.

Highly grounding stones: Black tourmaline, Carbon quartz, Galena, Obsidian, Jet, Onyx.

Principles for the Synergy of Melanin and Sacred Stones

Principle One:

Explore the biochemistry of melanin, then correspond to elements within the mineral kingdom.

As stated in Part One, the key biocrystalline molecule present in the human body is melanin. Melanin is a:

- A super-conductor of naturally occurring high frequency radiation and neural transmissions.
- A semiconductor of sound and heat energy.
- A conductor of the body's ionic charge.
- A resonator of visible light.

Melanin means 'Black amino' and is a color pigment composed of a hydrocarbon chain which has various amino (nitrogen-based) compounds attached to it. **It is carbon that gives melanin its Blackness.** Carbon is the organizing molecule that gives melanin its structure. It is carbon that gives melanin the ability to absorb energy and bind with other molecules while retaining stability and coherence.

Beyond carbon, there are two other elements that are important to the structure of melanin: copper and sulfur.

Copper is incorporated into the melanin molecule through the amino acid tyrosine. Tyronsinase is an organometallic amino compound that is organized around carbon, nitrogen, and copper. This amino acid is:

- the catalyst for melanin reproduction, and
- the amino compound that facilitates melanin's ability to conduct many Electro-magnetic frequencies.

Sulfur is incorporated into the melanin molecule through the amino compound cysteine. Cysteine is an amino compound that is organized around sulfur, nitrogen, and carbon. This amino acid facilitates melanin's heat and energy transference. In other words, it allows melanin to create or release heat as is needed for the body. Cysteine also cleanses and purifies melanin by 'burning off' toxic elements that have been absorbed within melanin.

The biochemistry of melanin indicates that there are at least three important elements necessary for maintenance of healthy melanin - Carbon, Copper, and Sulfur. Stones that contain these elements may be used as tools for harmonizing and refining how these elements are incorporated and maintained within melanin. [1]

The harmonizing is possible because stones that contain carbon, copper, or sulfur are in **resonant affinity** with melanin. Resonant affinity means 'like vibration'. When things are in resonant affinity, it means that they share the same frequencies and are joined in a unified energy field. For example, when a radio is tuned into a radio station, it is in resonant affinity with the station's broadcast antennae. Both the radio and the broadcast antennae are resonating the signal, and the radio is connected to the antennae through the broadcast signal.

Resonant affinity allows for mutual harmonic correspondence. In other words, through resonant affinity, two things can harmonize, refine, and realign one another. Through resonant affinity, stones that contain carbon, copper, or sulfur can harmonize, refine, and realign melanin. Each element refines melanin in its own way.

Carbon based stones tend to improve melanin's ability to absorb energy and bind elements, yet still retain a balanced, healthy structure. This gives carbon-based stones anti-carcinogenic, anti-aging, anti-mutagenic properties.

Some carbon-based stones include: Aragonite, Calcite, Carbonite, Carbon Quartz, Smoky Quartz, Diamond, Magnesite, Malachite, Melanite, Rhodochrosite, and Smithsonite.

Copper-based stones tend to electrify melanin. Copper tends to increase melanin's ionic potential, and stimulates melanin to produce an abundance of free electrons for the body. Copper-based stones also stimulate melanin production. Some powerful copper-based stones include: Azurite Chalcopyrite, Chrysacolla, Copper, Covellite, Cuprite, Dioptase, Malachite, Tetrahedite and Turquoise.

Sulfur based stones tend to cleanse and purify melanin. These stones also facilitate melanin's ability to transform heat into physical energy and visa versa. Sulfur based stones include: Cobaltite, Gypsum, Lazurite (Lapis Lazuli), Marcasite, Pyrite, Sulfur.

Principle Two

Skin melanin, perspiration, and certain metals create energy which melanin then converts into metabolic energy for the body.

In other words, ionic exchange occurs when electrolytes within sweat come into contact with metals adorned as jewelry. Melanin absorbs the ions exchanged in the process and turns it into food for the body. Details of some common metals worn as jewelry are as follows:

GOLD: Gold is an elemental metal which is very electrifying. It provides a catalytic, positive charge to the body when interacting with melanin, sweat, and sunlight.

SILVER: Silver is an elemental metal that is magnetic in polarity. Worn with gold or copper, an electromagnetic polarity is established. The result is a low-voltage current conducted through skin melanin. The melanin may then transform this energy into nourishment for the body.

COPPER: Copper has basically the same electromagnetic qualities as gold, but has the extra benefit of being in resonant affinity with copper-based melanin. Wearing copper jewelry feeds and nourishes melanin with one of its central compounds.

HEMATITE: Hematite is a metallic compound of iron and oxygen. Hematite means "blood stone," and recognizing that iron and oxygen are two component elements in blood, it is clear how hematite received its name. When interacting with melanin, sweat, and sunlight, hematite catalyzes the assimilation of iron and oxygen into the blood, thus strengthening the entire physical system.

PYRITE: Pyrite is a metallic compound which means "Fire stone." It is an iron-sulfite. As stated, iron is a central element of blood. Sulfur is the central element in the amino compound cysteine, a biopolymer component of melanin. When pyrite interacts with melanin, sweat, and sunlight, it electrifies, energizes, cleanses and fortifies both blood and melanin.

Principle Three

Striated stones have the potential to channel energy into the neuro-melanin structures deep within the central nervous system.

Striated Stones have parallel grooves recessed down the length of the stone. These parallel grooves create channels on the stone. These channels can focus large amounts of energy in one linear direction. This feature makes striated stones well suited for channeling energy deep into the physical body (into the spinal column, for example).

These stones are excellent for 'grooving' healing energies into the neural-melanin that lay deep within central nervous system. Used regularly, striated stones strengthen the nervous system so that it can conduct higher and more intense neural frequencies for longer duration without showing signs of stress.

Moreover, what we know as ESP (Extra-Sensory Perception) is actually LSP (Latent Sensory Perception). Latent means dormant or unawake. Everybody has the potential to sense unseen realities, but the skill has to be awakened. Being able to tune into unseen energies involves activating and awakening mind-powers that are centered in melanin plexus structures located throughout the spinal column. Down the length of the spinal column are ganglia of nerves, also known as nerve plexus centers. These nerve structures are highly melanated neural networks that assist the brain in coordination of the physical body. Striated stones, because of the highly focused, intense energy they emit, are the perfect tools to stimulate and activate these melanin plexus centers in the central nervous system.

Specific striated stones are as follows:

Tourmaline: Tourmaline manifests in a variety of colors, the most common being black, green, red, and watermelon (green, red, and clear). Tourmaline is pyro-electric potential, and discharges ionic charges when exposed to heat or flame.

Selenite: Selenite is a fragile stone in the gypsum family. The clarity of striated selenite is the most spectacular of the mineral nation; its ability to reflect and refract light even exceeds clear quartz crystal. Selenite has affinity with the element selenium, which is a vital component of the pineal gland. Excellent for balancing mind functions related to that gland.

Kyanite: A sky blue stone with pale white streaks, kyanite is one of the most highly charged stones in the striated family. The blue energy is cooling and calming to the body, yet the high-energy nature of the stone is invigorating. Holding kyanite or laying it on the body is a good way to relax and recharge. Or, one can use the stone as a wand to direct energy into a specific body area.

Kunzite: A soft pink, translucent, striated stone, kunzite is for ushering the pink ray of self-love and self-forgiveness into the most hardened heart.

Topaz: Topaz can channel a strong beam of ionic light from the crown of the head throughout the entire spinal column. The color of the light depends on the color of the topaz used. The most common colors of topaz are gold and blue.

Danburite: A highly translucent stone that also has complex terminations in conjunction with striations, Danburite is similar to topaz in that it channels radiant light deep into the spinal column.

Principle Four:

Quartz Crystal enhances melanin's ability to perform as a multi-spectrum conductor.

Recall from Part One that melanin is a:
- Super-conductor of high frequency electromagnetic radiation.
- A semi-conductor of sound and heat energy.
- Conductor of the body's ionic charge
- A resonator of visible light

Comparing the energy potentials of clear quartz crystal and melanin, interesting similarities and contrasts exist. Clear Quartz crystal is a:
- Super-conductor of the high frequency electromagnetic radiation.
- A semi-conductor of power frequencies
- Conductor of visible light and infrared radiation
- A resonator of all forms of radio waves

The synergistic application of melanin and quartz crystal is the foundation for a spiritual technology for the new millennium. Combining these two multi-spectrum conductors is the way for people of color to harmonize and harness the full spectrum of vibrations within creation. Specific applications are explored in the following sections.

NTU: African-Centered Psychotherapy and Re-centering Awareness with Sacred Stones

NTU

In 1972, an African-American psychologist named Wade Nobles published an article entitled 'African Philosophy: Foundations for Black Psychology.' This article launched a watershed within the study of African-American mental health because it spelled out for the first time the idea that:

- There is a specific African worldview; and

- Psychological concepts and therapeutic methods for African-Americans must be rooted in the African worldview to effectively address the present mental health challenges resulting from enslavement and colonization.

For the next two decades, Nobles and other members of the Association of Black Psychologist, notably Na'im Akbar, Daudi Azibo, Linda Myers and James Baldwin reclaimed and revitalized an African-centered psychological framework. As Baldwin states, "African cosmology thus provides the conceptual-philosophical framework for African (Black) Psychology."

In line with this, the historical root of psychology was traced back to the Nile Valley. The Kemetic word *Sakhu* (soul, spirit) was identified as the root for the English word psyche (mind). Therefore, psychology is from the African perspective the study of spirit, not mind. The African Sakhu-logical approach to mental health is recognized as the original human psychology as well and the optimal approach to achieving complete mind-body-spirit health. (Akbar, 1985; Myers, 1988).

Nobles identified seven Kemetic components of the human spirit in 1986:

Ka	Awareness of Life
Ba	Breath of Life
Khaba	Emotional/Sensory Body
Akhu	Mental body/Intellect
Seb	Ancestral Body
Putah	Super-conscious Mind/Collective Mind
Atmu	Eternal Life Force

Nobles also identified a clear, concise African worldview based on seven core cultural perspectives of reality.

African Cultural Perspective of Reality

Nature of universe (Cosmology) The universe is one in being. Therefore, everything is interconnected and interdependent.

Nature of reality (Ontology) The nature of reality is spiritual. The ultimate reality is an unseen energy that permeates and sustains all things.

Criteria for Value Judgement (Axiology) There is a rhythmic, cyclical interaction of opposite, yet complimentary forces. Therefore, there is no good/bad; only good and greater good (Its all good).

Guiding Principles (Ethos) Oneness with nature and harmonious relationships within society are how humans should live.

Ideal vision of things (Ideology) There should be harmonious interaction with all people and the natural order of creation.

Ideas about order (Worldview)

Nature dictates social order. Right is might.

Sense of self (Identity)

The self is extended - personal identity is seen as part of a family, clan, nation and ancestors.

The African cultural perspective is viewed as the optimal cultural perspective for African people. An African person who operates out of this perspective of reality is culturally centered and mentally healthy. To the degree that the person's perspective of reality is counter to this optimal perspective, he/she will experience spiritual and health challenges. [2]

This clearly defined cultural perspective and other Sakhu-logical concepts gave birth to a powerful African-Centered therapeutic method: *NTU*. Frederick B. Phillips, Henry Gregory, and other clinical staff of the **Progressive Life Center** experientially developed *NTU* from clinical work in Baltimore, Md., and Washington, DC around 1990.

NTU (pronounced 'into') is a Bantu/Central African name of the unifying force of the universe. This universal force is considered the essence of life and the healing force of nature. The goals of *NTU* therapy are to align people to the natural order of creation, and bring people into a harmonious relationship with the life essence of the universe (*NTU*).

NTU therapy has six characteristics as outlined by Phillips (1990):

1. **Spiritually Oriented:** The fact that the ultimate nature of reality is spiritual is honored and recognized. The task of *NTU* therapy is to clarify and align the recipient with his/her own spiritual belief system.

2. **Family Focused:** Participants in *NTU* therapy do not participate as individuals; the entire family is involved in the therapeutic process.

3. **Culturally Centered:** *NTU* is the optimal psychotherapeutic approach for people of African descent. However, because it is based on the original human psychology, it is appropriate for people of all races. When the participants are of other cultural origins, the therapist should assume the perspective of humble student and always be culturally sensitive.

4.　**Competency Based:** Focuses on the strengths of the participants, not deficits or problems. Uncovers what the client does well and builds upon it.

5.　**Holistic:** Addresses the Mind, Body, and Spirit of the participants.

6.　**Values Driven:** Promotes the Nguzo Saba as the healthy value system for African people.

Within *NTU* therapy, healing is viewed as a natural process. Wounds heal by themselves when the proper condition is created to nurture the process. The *NTU* therapist facilitates the healing process by creating the proper conditions for healing to occur. These conditions are achieved by establishing a relationship based on four guiding principles:

1.　**Harmony:** Moving with the flow of life; Union of mind, body and spirit.

2.　**Balance:** Acknowledging the polarity (positive and negative) in life and finding meaning in it all.

3.　**Interconnectedness:** Acknowledging that all things are interconnected and interrelated. Interconnectedness is experienced as love: a healing force/spirit/energy that is shared in the therapeutic relationship.

4.　**Authenticity:** Being true to oneself: Accessing the inner Self. Following the voice within and thus 'keeping it real'.

When a therapeutic relationship is established based upon these principles, the therapist then becomes a channel through which NTU (the universal healing force experienced as love) may heal. Therefore, the essential nature of therapy is vibrational, and to an African person, an effective therapy session is a vibrational experience. Henry Gregory, a co-creator of NTU and therapist at the Progressive Life Center (1996) states that:

> The therapist is a facilitator or conduit of the healing process. Therapy is the occasion for healing. The therapist creates the atmosphere and condition in which healing occurs and in direct proportion to his/her atonement to universal energy, channels healing energy (NTU). All

therapy at its essence is vibrational, as is all other experience. The purity and intensity of the healing is relative to the relational connection, the depth of wounding experience and the efforts of the participants. The conscious NTU psychotherapist is centered and uses his/her ability to tap into the life force to amass a quantity of energy that is shared with the client in the exploration of problems and solutions. Ideally, the client assumes more of the responsibility for gathering and maintaining the energy as the therapeutic process moves from dependence toward independence. [3]

NTU and Sacred Stones

Sacred Stones can greatly enhance the vibrational experience of Ntu therapy. Crystals can augment NTU healing in three specific ways:

Crystals can increase the intensity of NTU channeling through the therapist.

Translucent Stones allow the light of NTU to channel through: Clear quartz and Danburite are two effective translucent stones. Clear quartz when worn on the body acts as a beacon of shining NTU, as well as augments the therapist' ionic energy within his/her aura/energy field. It is the intense ionic charge within a person's aura that makes him/her radiant. A discharge of these ions occur as the therapists channels NTU to the client, thus intensifying the client's experience of feeling the healing force of universal love flow to them.

Danburite has a similar effect as clear quartz, but is actually more intense because in addition to being translucent, it is also striated and terminated. Danburite makes the therapist a bright beacon of NTU. Danburite also strengthens the nervous system of the therapist, thus allowing for him/her to manage the various crises of their clientele without accumulated stress or burn out.

Phosphorus stones illuminate the thoughts and words of the therapist. Recall that phosphorus means 'light producer', and it is the brain's consumption of phosphorus that empowers humans to think, memorize, visualize, and reason. Wearing phosphorus stones can facilitate clear, coherent thought and concise yet moving words. Phosphorus stones also facilitate the ability to think quickly and respond to immediate/presenting concerns. Apatite, Lazulite, and turquoise contain phosphorus.

Green stones foster peace, harmony and feelings of One Love within the therapist. The color green is associated with love, and activates the heart. Wearing green stones gives the therapist's aura a green hue, which the client experiences as a loving sensation. Adventurine, Antigorite, Malachite, Emerald, Chrysacolla, Jade, Apatite are powerful green stones.

Sacred stones can be given as gifts to strengthen the therapeutic bond and relational connection.

The power of giving is healing. The power of giving and sharing sacred stones is remarkably healing. People tend to truly appreciate the gift of a sacred stone, and count it as a valued personal treasure. A one-dollar piece of agate, quartz, or amethyst may buy your way into the most hardened heart and secure an open, sincere, trusting therapeutic relationship. Any semi-precious stone would work in this fashion. However, think wisely about the nature of the stone you are sharing and the nature of the person. You would not want to share a fiery red stone with an aggressive, belligerent, explosive person. Nor would you want to share a dark blue stone with a melancholy, depressed person with the 'blues'. (For more information on how to choose an appropriate gift stone, refer to *Re-centering and Healing African Families and Communities with Sacred Stones.*)

Crystals can align the client with the natural order of creation.

The same gifts that secured a trusting relationship also work to align the client while the therapist is not present. Natural crystals embody the natural order of creation. Crystals resonate the vibration of alignment, and bring people who come to possess them into harmonious living with the universal force of NTU and the natural order. Clear quartz crystal and optical clear calcite are two stones well suited for universal alignment. These stones align the total person, regardless of the roots of the person's mal-alignment.

Re-Centering

As stated, the African cultural perspective is viewed as the optimal cultural perspective for African people. An African person who operates out of this perspective of reality is culturally centered and mentally healthy. To the degree that the person's perspective of reality is counter to this optimal perspective, he/she will experience spiritual and mental health challenges. They will suffer from what African psychologist's such as Daudi Azibo define as *cultural misorientation*, also known as *African Sakhulogical misorientation.*

Examples of cultural misorientation, as well as the stones that impel realignment and re-centering are as follows:

Cosmological Misconception:

The universe is composed of unrelated objects. Independent and separate entities constitute the universe. There is no direct interconnection between things.

Behaviors:
- Pollution of environment;
- Destruction of life;
- Selfishness / Self-Centeredness;
- Unwillingness to serve others;
- Theological misorientation, defined as the practicing of a religion that is incongruent with African-centered history and spirituality. Examples are: Believing God is an external force instead of an internal force; Symbolizing Black as evil and White as good; Believing human nature is inherently sinful instead of inherently divine, Believing salvation and divinity come after death; fear of ancestral homage, etc.

Recentering Stones: These stones tend to break down thought structures that prevent one from feeling the connectedness of all things, as well as feel the Divine within. Elestial quartz, Amethyst, Sugilite, Lapis Lazuli, Malachite, Sodalite, Phenakite, Meteorites.

Ontological Misconception:

The ultimate reality is material. If one can not see, touch, feel, or measure something, then it does not exist.

Behaviors:

- Materialistic depression, which is basing personal happiness on the acquisition or loss of material possessions.
- Atheism and lack of faith;
- Lack of inherent Self-worth, because the unseen Spirit within is not acknowledged. Lack of inherent Self Worth is the foundation of self-hatred, negative and degrading profile of the Self. Also associated is low self-esteem, and dependence upon non-African standards and definitions of the Self. Dependence upon non-African definitions of the Self tend to lead to physical mutilation of hair, skin, and body to fit a non-African aesthetic.

Recentering Stones: These stones tend to impel one to know God within and balance material and spiritual values. Elestial quartz, pyrite (fool's gold), Celestite, Azurite, Kyanite, Adventurine, Phenakite, Herkimer diamonds, Selenite, Optical clear calcite, Clear Quartz, Apatite, Serpentine.

Axiological Misconception:

Opposing forces are antagonistic. One force must always conquer and overcome the other.

Behaviors:

- Black-on-Black crime;
- Sexism, spousal abuse, and poor male/female relations;
- Dysfunctional family structure,

- Racism
- Sexual misorientation (sexual relations that are not natural -order - consistent);
- Viewing competition as the means by which self worth is defined and validated.
- Poor conflict solving; fighting, battling, war and strife.

Recentering Stones: These stones tend to balance and harmonize the polar opposition of life on Earth. Elestial Quartz, Twin quartz, Double-terminated quartz, Red calcite, Tourmaline, Labradorite, Flourite octahedrons, Magnetite octahedrons, Hematite, Moki marbles, Boji stones, Garnet, Goddess clay concretions, Aragonite, Linghams, Red Quartz.

Ethical Misconception:

One should live by conquering nature and natural people. Might is right, and the mightiest set the social order.

Behaviors:
- Living in urban environments cut off from and unaware of the natural order.
- Viewing African traditional culture as primitive and uncivilized.
- Associating civilization with the conquering of nature.
- Eating diet of denatured, refined, and processed food. Excessive meat eating and carnivorous disposition.
- Use of force and violence to resolve conflict.

Recentering Stones: These stones impel one to live in oneness with nature and people of the world. Quartz cluster, Geodes, Stones within their matrix, Mica, Schist, Clear Quartz, Goddess Clay concretions, Citrine, Amber, Cowry shell, Serpentine.

Ideological misconception:

Survival of the fittest is how things should be. The fittest have the right to exploit nature and natural people to accumulate possessions.

Behaviors:

- Poor community development;
- Lack of viable social institutions;
- Inability to promote Umoja (unity);
- Materialistic depression;
- Insensitivity to social challenges such as famine, starvation, and poverty;
- Lack of collective consciousness;
- Remain divided and conquered.

Recentering Stones: These stones refine ideals and give harmonious purpose to life. Elestial quartz, Clear quartz, Amethyst, Obsidian, Malachite, Adventurine, Chrysacolla, Turquoise, Dioptase, Lepidolite, Quartz cluster, Moldavite tektite.

Mal-aligned Worldview:

Man is here to conquer nature. Man should not live in harmony with nature, but master and control nature. Man should live in an artificially created environment.

Behaviors:

- Physical disease of all sorts;
- Living in urban environments cut off from and unaware of the natural order.

- Urban Learner Syndrome in youth, which is viewing education process as irrelevant to the degree that the maladaptive behaviors prevents acquiring knowledge and/or survival skills.
- Youth and family relations out of order.
- Infertility, hyper-fertility, teen-age pregnancy.
- Dependent living upon technology which is beyond personal design or control.

Recentering Stones: These stones tend to reinforce and reestablish the natural order within a person. Elestial quartz, Clear quartz, Carnelian, Agates, Adventurine, Citrine, Gold Topaz, Tiger's Eye, Amethyst, Geodes, Quartz clusters.

Misoriented Identity:

The Self is individual in nature. The Self is not a part of a collective identity.

Behaviors:

- Disassociation with the collective, ancestral mind;
- Rugged individualism (me first mentality); 'me, myself, and I' attitude.
- Striving to live independent of nature, family, or racial group.

Within African people, striving towards independence leads to many personality disorders identified by European Psychology. (paranoia, anxiety, schizophrenia, nervous breakdown, depression, etc.)

Recentering Stones: These stones tend to broaden the definition of Self and make it more collective and encompassing. Quartz cluster, Geodes, Self-Healed quartz, Amethyst, Hematite, Bloodstone, Phenakite, Elestial quartz, Lepidolite, Sugilite, Azurite. [4]

These stones can be given to those participating in NTU therapy, or incorporated in layouts. Details of the art and science of layouts are included in *Bioresonance.*

NTU for the Masses

There is truly a mental health crises within the African-American community. The masses of Africans-in-America are misoriented - culturally and Sakhulogically. Mass realignment is needed if African-Americans are to achieve stable, harmonious communities for the future generations.

For the amount of healing that needs to occur, numerically speaking, it is almost impossible that the number of trained mental health professionals can effectively achieve individual/family/community mental health. This is considering all trained mental health professionals, not just African-centered practitioners who utilize NTU and other culturally relevant approaches. When African-Centered practitioners are considered alone, the chances of affecting realignment appear impossible. Truly, a broader approach to re-centering the mental health of the African-American community must be found.

This is why this survey of NTU and its potential synthesis with sacred stone sciences is presented - to empower African people to heal themselves, their families and communities. NTU, unlike Freudian and other Eurocentric approaches to mental health, is not invasive. It does not involve the therapist probing and psychoanalyzing the client's mind. NTU is relationship-based - the therapist builds a sacred relationship based on four spiritual principles.

One spiritual principle of the therapeutic relationship is authenticity. Authenticity, or 'keeping it real', implies encouraging the client to trust and be true to his/her inner Self. However, it also implies that NTU should occur in authentic, real life situations. Phillips (1990) views the Nguzo Saba - the Seven Principles - as the key to actualizing NTU within authentic, real life settings. He corresponds a Nguzo Saba Principle with authentic NTU techniques that are applied in family and community settings. The following is a chart that outlines Nguzo Saba principles, NTU key concepts, therapeutic tasks, and techniques. [5]

Principle	Key Concepts	Therapeutic Tasks	Techniques
Umoja (Unity)	Harmony Interdependence of life Unity is Natural	Experience closeness of being through group action Experience Interconnectedness	Rituals (libations. prayer, Afro drama, etc.) Self-Disclosure, Humor, Reframing Genogram
	High Value of Relationships	Awareness of Self-Barriers to Closeness	Being Real. Re-energize spiritually
Kujichagulia (Self Determination)	Empowerment	Cultural Awareness	Ugogram, Awareness Wheel, Rites of Passage Program
	Authenticity self-esteem	Awareness of Self Potential Positive Regard for self Awareness of Strength of Inner-Self (NTU) Awareness of Psychological Barriers	Guided Imagery, Peeling the Onion, Cultural, Informative, Creative Visualization

Principle	Key Concepts	Therapeutic Tasks	Techniques
Ujima (Collective Work Responsibility)	Balance	Balance "I" and "we"	Multi-Family Retreat, Kinship Karamu,
	Mutual Interdependence Extended Self Active Togetherness and Family	Experience NTU	Effective Communication Exercises, Family Drawing
	Collective Past, Present, and Future	Experience importance of self and others	Therapeutic Games. Modeling, Reframing
		Effective communications including accepting responsibility for correcting others	
Ujamaa (Cooperative Economics)	Mutual financial interdependence	Experience money as a tool, not a source of pleasure	Family Budget. Tracing of income and expenditures
	Shared wealth and resources	Awareness of multiple efforts that contribute to one's success	Guided Imagery Values Clarification Cooperative Ventures
	Balance	Sharing of resources to further health of extended self	
	Wealth and resources belong to all	Balancing money and communal responsibility	
	People before Profits		

Principle	Key Concepts	Therapeutic Tasks	Techniques
Nia (Purpose)	Authenticity	Experience our purpose through being NTU	Guided Imagery, Connection to our ancestors
	We each have a unique contribution		Relaxation exercises, Self Awareness
	Clear purpose has roots in identity	Relaxation and calmness	Exercises Cultural Awareness Exercises
	Provides Direction and Meaning to life	Awareness	
Kuumba (Creativity)	Authenticity	Balance feeling and sensing with thinking	Action Techniques, Role Plays
	There is a Creative spirit (NTU) Within everyone	Trust inner-self	Visualization Humor Reframing and relabeling
	We have the Capacity to bring Into being a New Reality	Experience being in harmony and learning to re-balance	
	Creative labor is Self-defining, self Developing, and Self-confirming	Feel comfortable with allowing inner self to organize physical being	
Imani (Faith)	Harmony Interconnectedness	Alignment of ourselves in Harmony and balance with our essence (NTU)	Prayer Spiritual Readings Unity Circles Affirmations Meditation Relaxation Nature Study

The challenge to the reader is to **be** the broader approach to re-centering the mental health of the African-American community by:

- Re-aligning and centering yourself with the help of sacred stones.

- Gain a working knowledge of the principles, goals, and techniques of NTU therapy; either by reading research on the approach (bibliography included at end of book), or by corresponding directly with the Progressive Life Center. Their telephone number is (202) 842-4570.

- Wear transluscent stones and illuminate NTU to your family and community while engaged in the tasks and techniques outlined in the proceeding chart .

- Share stones with family and community members, noting in what ways they need to be realigned to be in accord with the African Cultural Perspective of reality.

May NTU be with you!

Harmonizing Families and Communities with Sacred Stones

Within the African Cultural Perspective outlined in the proceeding chapter, African identity is characterized as extended. That is: personal identity is seen as part of a family. 'I am because we are, and we are because I am' sums up the sentiment. It runs counter to the Western notion of individualism, or 'I am that I am'. Based on the African perspective of self-identity, in order to harmonize and heal an individual, his/her family must be healed.

The African family is truly extended; because within African culture, family extends beyond human relations. Nature and God are part of the African family. (See diagram on opposite page.)

The preceding diagram also gives insight into the relationship of sacred stones and humanity. Sacred stones are an embodiment of Earth Elementals or Spirits of Nature. They are part of our family. The role of Earth stones within the family is to provide humans with nurturing guidance and protection.

As family, Earth stones want humanity to be healthy and happy. As such, they are like a loving grandmother who unconditionally showers her offspring with abundance, love, nourishment, and guidance. This makes them invaluable gifts for healing ourselves.

The following is an outline as to how one can share the gift of healing with all of his/her relations. Assuming that most readers are adults, adulthood will be the primary reference within the outline. The thrust of the outline is to provide suggested stones that will heal the family member as well as harmonize the relationship.

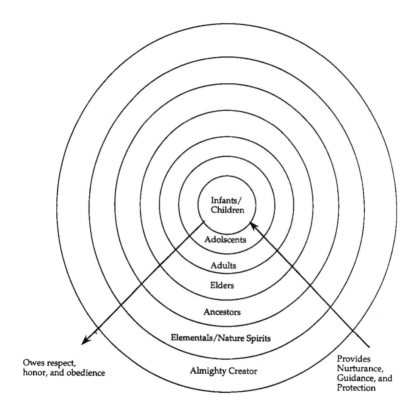

Infants/
Children

Adolscents

Adults

Elders

Ancestors

Elementals/Nature Spirits

Almighty Creator

Owes respect,
honor, and obedience

Provides
Nurturance,
Guidance, and
Protection

ALL I-n-I RELATIONS FROM THE AFRICAN CULTURAL PERSPECTIVE

Adult & Child Relations

For Infants and Children:

Clear Quartz - Helps little ones be 'bright' by infusing ionic-energy into their being. Surround their environment with quartz and let them sleep with quartz. Make sure stone is large enough to not be a choking hazard. Also make sure child's breathing will not be obstructed or head wedged by stone.

Moldavite Tektites and other Meteorites - Helps child fully adjust to earth and be mentally, physically, and spiritually healthy. Place over the 'soft spot' of newborns and infants; and allow children to wear as talisman/amulet/charm.

For Adults:

Blue Calcite and Celestite - Builds patience and understanding. Sleep with it.

Green Tourmaline and Green Serpentine - Gives vitality and endurance enough for parent to be able to hang with little one's energy all day. Wear in pockets.

Rose quartz, Kunzite, and Rhodochrosite - Invokes the ability to forgive and forget. Increases compassion and allows parent to share more love with little ones. Heals the 'inner child'.

Adult & Adolescent Relations

For Adolescents:

Amethyst - Lay over the '1st eye' region. Helps balance pituitary secretions during the transition of puberty.

Chrysacolla - Allows young people to communicate feelings more clearly and with less resentment or frustration. Wear daily.

Citrine - Allows young people to assimilate life experiences without having to go through trial and tribulation over and over (and over) again.

Gold Topaz - Wards off procrastination and promotes good study habits.

Meteorites and Tektites - Increases mental strength and awakens dormant mind powers.

Adolescents may need the stone in a form of jewelry so that they can wear it and still be 'cool'.

For Adults:

Smoky Quartz - Allows parent to release money and other financial assistance without attaching guilt-ridden strings.

Azurite, Lapis Lazuli, and Elestial Quartz - Fosters an understanding of the transitions and cycles of life, which allows parent to let youth go through adolescent challenges without experiencing too much anxiety.

Dioptase and Rose Quartz - These stones promote unconditional love and acceptance. They encourage forgiveness and nurturing.

Adult & Adult Relations

Relating to Self:

Clear quartz, Phenakite, & Moldavite tektite - These stones allow one to know, identify, relate, and master all aspects of self. Wear daily. Balance with grounding stones (Black tourmaline, Hematite, Pyrite, Carnelian, Moki marbles).

Window quartz - Encourages Self-analysis and introspection. Helps refine character and moral fiber.

Flourite, Calcite, Magnetite octahedrons - Refines personal habits and strengthens the foundation of one's thought-forms. Gives one a balanced perspective of life.

Intimate Relations:

Malachite, Dioptase, rose quartz, Kunzite, a Rhodochrosite - Allows one to share love and intimate feelings without past emotional pain, trauma, and hurt getting in the way. Lay over heart, Solar plexus and reproductive areas.

Elestial quartz - allows soul mates to recall past life experiences they shared together. In tandem, hold elestial in hands and face one another while breathing in unison.

Moki Marbles, Boji stones, Shiva Linghams, Moonstone, and Goddess clay concretions - Promote balance and equity between the sexes. Allows men to harmonize their feminine aspect of self, and allows women to harmonize the masculine aspect of themselves. Brings happiness and laughter into relationship.

Franklinite, Tiger's Eye, and Carnelian - Strengthens the reproductive organs and enhances enjoyable intimate connections.

Associate Relations:

Clear quartz; Blue quartz, Chrysacolla - Promotes clear, effective communication. Minimizes misunderstandings.

Garnet, Danburite, Sulfur, Gold topaz, Tiger's Eye - creates an attractive radiance and promotes appeal.

Black Tourmaline - Protection from inharmonious intentions of associates.

Adult & Elder Relations

For Adults:

Same stones that are recommended for Adult & Child relations (remember, once a man, twice a child).

For Elders:

Bloodstone, Hematite, Pyrite - Strengthens blood and the body. Reverses debilitating conditions.

Copper - Relieves arthritis conditions and promotes flexibility of limbs and joints.

Lepidolite - Contains natural lithium - assists in memory loss, Alzheimer's disease, and related conditions.

All Flourites and Calcites - Keeps the mind strong. Promotes retention of long and short-term memory.

Carnelian & Elestials - Helps with the transition to the afterlife. Removes fear and doubts.

Adult & Ancestor Relations

Create an ancestral altar. Collect photos and belongings of the ancestors to be communed with. Find a communal place in the home and arrange these things in an orderly way on a mat, mud cloth fabric, Kente, or some other sacred African print. Routinely place a candle, a glass of water, and flowers on the altar. Occasionally share an evening meal and place a plate of dinner upon the altar. Be open to offer whatever the ancestors guide you to do in order to facilitate clear communion. Surround the altar with **clear quartz crystals**. A **large quartz cluster** is ideal as a centerpiece. The quartz will become a home of light for your spiritual family. The quartz will also act as a 'microphone' of the ancestors, and they will commune their love, guidance, and protection through the stones when you spend quiet time in front of the altar. You will hear their words as an inner voice speaking in your mind.

You may be moved to consecrate (set apart and declare sacred) one stone to a particular ancestor, making the quartz their exclusive home and microphone. It may have a place on the altar, but may be small enough to travel with you at certain times. These stones usually appear to have deep inner worlds when one peers into them. They may have rainbow inclusions, milky clouds that appear to shift in time; they may even contain an image of a face or eye. These are personal stones that are not to be handled by others unless they are close family.

Black tourmaline, Lodestone, Magnetite and Moki marbles centrally or symmetrically placed on the altar helps ground the communion, making the inner voice louder, mental focus sharper, concentration longer, and the meditation a total body experience.

Adult & Earth Elemental Relations

Find a natural place relatively untouched by 'development' (devil-up-ment). Routinely clean area of any pollution or trash to show right intention to the elementals that live in the area. Find a large tree with an opening in the trunk. Place a large piece of **clear quartz** in the opening and then routinely spend quiet time sitting by the tree. The quartz is a gift to the elementals. It should remain in the tree. The elementals will commune their nurturing guidance, and protection through the stone. Reciprocate with respect, honor, and obedience.

Keep the area clean and adopt an overall environmental friendly awareness. Recycle, clean litter, be mindful of fuel usage, limit water consumption, protect trees and grow vegetation. Do all you can to rejuvenate the natural world, even make peace with the insect nation. As you become ecologically active and are a regenerating force for mother Earth, the nature spirits of your crystal tree will reveal environmental friendly technologies that will afford a high quality of living yet be in harmony with the planet.

Adult & Divine Relations

Always remember that your body is the biocrystalline temple of the living Jah (The One Most High God). It is easier to access God within your inner world than in any church, synagogue, mosque, ashram, etc. Do not defile the temple with dead flesh, drugs or alcohol. Exercise regularly. Feed the mind with inspirational scripture daily. Avoid behaving out of anger, fear, and aggression. Wear **Clear quartz crystal**, **Phenakite**, and **Moldavite tektite** daily! These stones will align your consciousness into harmonious oneness with the Almighty! Each thought, word, action, and deed will be divinely inspired. God's presence in your life will be pronounced. The Spirit of All will appear to permeate experiences. Synchronicity, or the meaning of all inter-relations will be made manifest. An attitude of love, gratitude, and appreciation will overcome personality.

If these stones are too elevating, and light-headedness, clouded perception, or disassociation with the material plane occurs, ground yourself with **Black tourmaline**, **Hematite**, or **Carnelian**.

African Spirituality and Sacred Stones

In the historical survey of sacred stones in part two, it was established that sacred stones are an integral part of African spiritual expression. Throughout time and space, it appears that sacred stones have been the cornerstone of African Spirituality. It is safe to say that almost every diverse ethnic group on the African continent and the African Diaspora use some form of sacred stones as a part of their spiritual expression.

The primary reason that the use of sacred stones appears universal in African spiritual expression is that all African people share common ancestry, from which was inherited a common spiritual base. This common spiritual base has metamorphosed throughout time and space, appearing as a multitude of different religions. However, one spiritual essence is common to all African religions.

Cheikh Anta Diop, the great Senegalese scholar and author of *The Cultural Unity of Black Africa*, recognized that within the African world, there is a "profound cultural unity still alive beneath the deceptive appearance of cultural heterogeneity". [1]

In other words, there are aesthetic differences between different African groups. Part of these aesthetic differences includes apparently different expressions of spirituality. At face value, the Neter of Kemet, the Abosum of the Akan, the Archangels of the Coptic Church, the Orisha of the Yoruba, and the Divine Names of Judaism and Islam appear as different and even contradictory 'religions'.

However, beneath the veil of symbolic differences is a cosmological unity. Cosmology literally means study (science) of the universe. Traditionally, African spiritual expression is based on cosmological principle, and African spirituality is a natural blend of science and religion.

The traditional African science of the universe recognizes:
- The One God Creator of the Universe
- A Heavenly Host, usually seven 'Great' Spirits, as well as various orders of minor Heavenly Spirits
- Ancestral Spirits of the Clan or Nation
- Nature Spirits, or Elementals of the Earth

By corresponding the common symbolic elements within various African spiritual systems, the parallel Arch-Types of the Neter of Kemet, Abosum of the Akan, Archangels of the Coptic Christian Church and Islam, the Orisha of the Yoruba, the Deities of Voudon and the Divine Names of Judaism are presented. Appropriate sacred stones for invoking and harmonizing The One God Force and the Seven Great Heavenly Host of each tradition is included. The corresponding days of the week, color, metal, celestial planet, and chakra is included as well.

(NOTE: Chakras are energy vortex centers that run along the center meridian of the body. Each chakra is associated with a mind power, or mind-body manifestation. They are arranged in an octave, and each has a corresponding musical tone and color of the light spectrum. Chakra science is explored more in-depth in Bioresonance.)

The Form-Energy Dynamics of a healthy chakra system.

Arch-Type:

The One God-Creator of the Universe, The 'All Mighty' Most High God that is omniscient (All knowing), omnipotent (All power), and omnipresent (All places). The Universal God-Force, Creator of all that there is in existence.

Psycho-Spiritual Qualities: One Love, Heart-knowing, Total acceptance, Non partiality, Universal citizenship

Celestial Home:	Galactic Core
Day:	Everyday
Chakra:	All Chakras
Color:	All Colors
Kemetic (Neter):	Ra
Yoruba (Orisha):	Oladumare
Akan (Abosum):	Onyame
Haitian Voudon:	Dambhallah Wedo
Judeo-Christian:	Jah; Jahovia
Islamic:	Allah
Metal:	Every metal
Stones:	Every stone

Arch-Type:

The Heavenly Father who created hue-manity. He is the Ancient of Days, the 'Ancient of Ancients', the ruler and master of time.

As the ruler of time, he controls all life cycles. His age teaches wisdom, morality, ethics, humility, and calmness. He is associated with the process of crystallization, and his home is often quartz crystal.

Psycho-spiritual Qualities: Humility, Discipline, Obedience to cosmic order, Sacrifice and service, Work and duty, Burdens, Restrictions, Limits, Issues of timeliness, Reward for effort.

Celestial Home:	Saturn
Day:	Saturday
Chakra:	Crown Chakra
Color:	White
Neter:	Asar
Orisha:	Obatala
Abosum:	Amen
Voudon:	Brigitte
Divine Name:	Jahovia Elohim
ArchAngel:	Kassiel
Islamic Angel:	Ridwan
Metal:	Lead

Stones: Clear Quartz Crystal, Phenakite, Selenite, Optical Clear Calcite, Moldavite Tektite and other Meteorites, Apophyllite, Elestial Quartz, Galena, Danburite

Arch-Type:

The Divine Teacher who descended from Heaven to bring Humanity the gift of civilized living, knowledge, wisdom, and 'overstanding'. The teacher of science, religion, agriculture, astrology, and writing. Upholder and defender of truth, justice, righteousness, and harmony. The Lawgiver and righteous judge. Associated with mountains and high places.

Psycho-Spiritual Qualities: Practice of spirituality, Blessings, Justice, Fortune, Use of judgement, Grace, Knowledge, Wisdom, Overstanding, Social Standing

Celestial Home:	Jupiter
Day:	Thursday
Chakra:	1st Eye/Center of forehead
Color:	Purple
Neter:	Tehuti & Maat
Orisha:	Orunla
Abosum:	Yaw
Voudon:	Adoum-Guidi
Divine-Name:	El
ArchAngel:	Sahkiel
Islamic Angel:	Israfil
Metal:	Tin/Brass

Stones: Amethyst, Purple and Gold Flourite, Lapis Lazuli, Lepidolite, Sugilite, Amethyst Elestials, Sodalite, Azurite

Arch-Type:

The Divine Messenger and ruler of the roads of life. Embodies free will and the power of decision-making. Represents the crossroads where decisions are made and the doorways through which destiny is fullfilled. Rules communication, commuting, and communion. The 'Word' of God; or the principle of vibration as a creative force in forming reality. Associated with the air, atmosphere, and wind.

Psycho-Spiritual Qualities: Mental acuity, Memory Perception, Concentration, Focus, Decision-making, Analysis, Free will, Speech & word-choice.

Celestial Home:	Mercury
Day:	Wednesday
Chakra:	Throat Chakra
Colors:	Blue & Yellow
Neter:	Sebek
Orisha:	Ellegua
Abosum:	Aku
Voudon:	Legba
Divine-Name:	Elohim Tsaboath
ArchAngel:	Raphael
Islamic Angel:	Azrael
Metal:	Mercury

Stones: Blue Quartz, Chrysacolla, Turquoise, Blue Agate, Celestite, Indicolite, Blue Calcite, Aquamarine, Blue Topaz

Arch-Type:

The Loving Son that illuminates creation with stunning radiance. His bright force appears in a flash, revealing what was unknown and battling the force of darkness. He is the Divine Avenger, the conqueror of darkness and falsehood. Is associated with sunlight, rain, fertility, and sustaining life processes on Earth.

Psycho-Spiritual Qualities: Appearance, Personal radiance, Magnetism, Externalization of Personality, Self-Mastery, Health of Body, Sphere of Influence, and Illumination

Celestial Home:	Sun
Day:	Sunday
Chakra:	Heart Chakra
Color:	Gold, Pink
Neter:	Heru
Orisha:	Chango
Abosum:	Awusi
Voudon:	Ogou-Chango
Divine-Name:	Jahovia Eloah
ArchAngel:	Mikael (Michael)
Islamic Angel:	Mika'Il
Metal:	Gold

Stones: Rose Quartz, Rhodochrosite, Kunzite, Dioptase, Malachite, and Pink Tourmaline

Arch-Type:

The goddess of love, beauty, music, harmony, sweet scents and foods. Rules the powers of sensuality and pleasure. Associated with fresh water rivers and streams. She also rules the rivers of the body: the bloodstream. As a result, she is associated with medicine, purification, and healing. She grants culture, art, grace, social skills, abundance and prosperity.

Psycho-Spiritual Qualities: Balance between material & spiritual values; Loving & harmonious relations; Balancing the pleasure principle; Grace, Charm, & Diplomacy.

Celestial Home:	Venus
Day:	Friday
Chakra:	Solar Plexus
Color:	Green & Gold
Neter:	Het-Heru
Orisha:	Oshun
Abosum:	Afi
Voudon:	Erzulie
Divine-Name:	Jahovia Tsaboath
ArchAngel:	Anuel
Islamic Angel:	Isma'Il
Metal:	Copper

Stones: Dioptase, All copper-based stones, Malachite, Green Tourmaline, Adventurine, Emerald, Copper, Citrine, Rutile Quartz, Gold Calcite, Gold, Tiger's Eye, Amber, Gold Topaz

Arch-Type:

Divine Will, expressed as the energy, force, and locomotion that keeps matter in motion. Associated with gravity, rotational, and orbital forces of earth. Lives in iron and is Electro-magnetic. Associated with everything yang, male, external. He rules over war, bloodshed, sacrifice, red things, and violence. He also rules tools, mines, and mining. It is he that surfaces the mineral resources of the inner-earth.

Psycho-Spiritual Qualities: Ambition, Motivation; Energy level, Desires, Ability, Survival skills, Competitive and combative urges

Celestial Home:	Mars
Day:	Tuesday
Chakra:	Sacral chakra / Pro-creative region
Color:	Red
Neter:	Heru-Khuti
Orisha:	Ogun
Abosum:	Bena
Voudon:	Ogou-Feraille
Divine-Name:	Elohim Ghebor
ArchAngel:	Khamael
Islamic Angel:	Munkir
Metal:	Iron

Stones: Carnelian, Red Quartz, Red Tourmaline, Bloodstone, Pyrite, Hematite, Red Calcite, Garnet, and Ruby

Arch-Type:

The Moon Mother of Hue-manity. The principle of motherhood, the womb, the Queen of Mothers. She is associated with oceans and salt-water seas. The Divine Nurturer and provider. The suckler who nurses her offspring. Associated with feelings, emotions, sensitivity, intuition, and 'motherwit'.

Psycho-Spiritual Qualities: Sensitivity, Emotions, Inner-feelings, Moods, Nurturing of Self & others, Fertility, Birth & re-Birth, Intuition, Imagination, Psychic Power, Ebb & flow of life.

Celestial Home:	Moon
Day:	Monday
Chakra:	Root Chakra / Coccyx
Color:	Black
Neter:	Auset
Orisha:	Yemenjah
Abosum:	Adwo
Voudon:	Aida Wedo
Divine Name:	EL Shaddai
ArchAngel:	Gabriel
Islamic Angel:	Jibril
Metal:	Silver

Stones: Moonstone, Opal, Sea Shell/Coral, Smokey Quartz, Silver, and Pearl, Black Tourmaline, Black Obsidian

Potential Applications

Some seeds of thought for invoking and harmonizing the spiritual forces with sacred stones:

- Hold stone while chanting name of the spiritual force on its corresponding day.

- Establish an altar with symbols of the spiritual force, articles sacred to the force, and corresponding stones.

- Wear or lay the stone that corresponds to the particular spiritual force on the corresponding chakra.

- Acquire two stones sacred to a particular spiritual force. Trod a pilgrimage to the natural elements associated with that spiritual force. Offer one stone to the elements, and pray that the second stone (which you are going to keep) can be a covenant stone that symbolizes the bond you share with that spiritual force. For example, to connect with the Moon Mother of All, one could take two moonstones to the ocean; preferably on a Monday, New, full, or quarter moon. Offer one stone to the ocean by tossing it in the water or leaving it at the wave break to be eaten by the tide. Ask the Moon Mother (who 'lives' in the ocean) to make the moonstone you are keeping to be a covenant stone. Dip the stone in the water to affirm the connection. The stone now embodies the relationship and connection between the moon mother and you.

- Create multimedia graphics artwork composed of symbols and articles sacred to spiritual force. Incorporate sacred stones.

- Attune yourself with the particular spiritual force and allow intuitive guidance to inspire you to do what is right and appropriate with the stones.

Survival In The Urban Toxic Zone

At the turn of the twentieth century, the industrial revolution was moving into full gear. The chance of a better life induced many of the African sharecroppers of the South and Caribbean to migrate to the big industrial cities of the North. The big cities offered them a way to physically move beyond the Southern plantation culture of chattel slavery. As a result, for the past one hundred years, there has been a process of urbanization occurring in Black American culture.

Escaping the South came at a cost: Urbanized Africans became disconnected from the Earth and nature. Standing on the verge of the twenty- first century, many African-American urban-dwellers are two to four generations removed from nature and the Earth. They do not grow their own food; till some soil; harvest natural resources from the forests and Earth. Instead, they live and die as consumers in the concrete jungles of North America. Most of the food consumed is refined, denatured, and processed. This situation has caused an epidemic of diseases and disorders within many African-American urban communities.

To compound the situation, many of the industries that are the source of employment in urban centers are also a main source of environmental pollution. Continuous discharge of industrial waste has caused a bio-chemical breakdown to occur within the ecological fabric of most urban centers. Toxins and poisonous chemicals in the land, water, air, food chain, and immediate living environment are inducing diseases and health disorders at an alarming rate. The toxic living conditions are the primary factor in the dramatic increase in cancer, sterility, and birth defects; and are contributing factors to immune-deficient disorders, ranging from the common cold and influenza, to AIDS.

African-American urban communities are being hit hardest by these health challenges. John Harris and Nana Imhotep Gary Byrd, creators of the Resource Guide, *'Escape From the Toxic Zone: A System of*

Survival', explores the health crisis occurring among Africans in American cities. [1]

The African-American community is deeply engulfed in a 'Toxic Zone'. A silent health crisis that staggers the imagination has claimed its share of the disempowered. African-Americans are victims of widespread environmental poisoning which yields chronic diseases such as cancer, heart disease, high blood pressure, AIDS, immune dysfunction, and diabetes.

Deadly respiratory ailments such as lung disease, TB, emphysema, and asthma are disproportionate to the numbers in the general population, asthma alone is recorded at nine (9) times the national average... Each day 122 African Americans will die from some form of cancer, and almost twice that number will be diagnosed with the dreaded disease. Cancer of the prostate is 30% higher in Black males than in the general population. Recent studies reveal that Black women will die from Breast cancer at a rate 2.5 times greater than white females.

Harris and Byrd cite the following key factors which influence the health of African-American urban dwellers:

Genetics: Constitutional strengths and weaknesses of Africans, with resulting environmental needs.

Diet: Eating foods that are denatured, refined, high in fat, pesticide ridden, preservative laden, full of chemical additives, filled with antibiotics and hormones.

Mental And Emotional Stress: Chronic anger, fear, grief, and other powerful emotions stresses the nervous system causing depressed immune response and other physical disorders.

Environmental Pollution: Pollutants in the air, water, soil, food, and immediate living environment contributes to disorders ranging from allergies to cancer.

Inappropriate Use Of Antibiotics And Vaccines: Disrupts the delicate balance of the body and fosters a variety of maladies, including ear infection, food allergies, and immune suppression.

Dental Factors: Mercury used in dental fillings are causing ailments that resemble multiple sclerosis, chronic fatigue syndrome, and autoimmune disorders.

Electro-Magnetic Fields: EMF's are harmful frequencies of radiation emitted by televisions, computer displays, electric wiring of homes, high voltage wiring, electrical appliances, cordless and cellular telephones, microwave ovens, even electric razors. The radiations these gadgets emit are considered Extra-Low Frequency (ELF), and they range in frequency from 30 to 100 cycles-per-second (hertz). ELF radiation is a factor in chronic stress, stunted or deformed cell growth and division, neuro-chemical and genetic alterations, immune system dysfunction, altered hormone production and biological cycles, acceleration of tumor growth, and cancer.

Geopathic Stress: Refers to illnesses caused by harmful vibrations from the Earth, such as radon gas. 30% to 50% of urban dwellers that are chronically ill exhibit signs of geopathic stress. Depression, violent mood swings, respiratory conditions, and abnormal sleep cycles are common to those afflicted.

Applications Of Sacred Stones To Address Each Cited Factor

GENETICS

DNA is composed of five basic elements: Carbon, Nitrogen, Hydrogen, Phosphorus, and Oxygen. Crystalline structures containing these elements tend to promote alignment of DNA.

Carbon Stones: Aragonite, Calcite, Carbonite, Carbon Quartz, Smoky Quartz, Diamond, Magnesite, Malachite, Melanite, Rhodochrosite, and Smithsonite.

Hydrogen Stones: Antigorite, Apatite, Apophyllite, Azurite, Childrenite, Chrysacolla, Dioptase, Epidote, Lazulite, Lepidolite, Malachite, Opal, Serpentine, Tourmaline, Tourquoise, Zoisite.

Phosphorus Stones: Amblygonite, Apatite, Brazilianite, Childrenite, Lazulite, Monazite, Pyromorphite, and Turquoise

Nitrogen Stones: Niter

Oxygen Stones: Agate, Albite, Antigorite, Apatite, Apophyllite, Aragonite, Azurite, Beryl, Calcite, Celestite, Childrenite, Chrysacolla, Corundum, Cuprite, Danburite, Dioptase, Franklinite, Hematite, Kyanite, Labradorite, Lazulite, Lazurite, Lepidolite, Limonite, Magnesite, Magnetite, Malachite, Olivine, Opal, Phenakite, Quartz, Rhodochrosite, Rhodonite, Rutile, Serpentine, Sodalite, Topaz, Tourmaline, Turquoise, Willemite, Zoisite

Clear Quartz Crystal: Quartz crystal and DNA are in resonant affinity' (they share like vibrations). Quartz crystal is a natural, mineralogical model of perfection for DNA to realign with. The quartz will 'tune' DNA into proper alignment and health.

Elestial Quartz: (Smoked, skeletal quartz) Programs DNA with knowledge/skill and information needed for ensured survival; "mystic revealer", which reveals volumes of knowledge locked within genetic code; connects person with space nations and citizens of the Hollow Earth (underworld). Reconstitutes the nervous system and melanin centers for superconductivity of angelic information.

DIET

Sodium, Hydrogen and Potassium are key elements in the digestive process. Crystalline structures with these elements tend to realign eating habits and digestive processes.

Potassium Stones: Adularia, Alunite, Apophyllite, Lepidolite, Leucite, Muscovite, Neptunite, Niter, Sanidine, and Sylvite

Sodium Stones: Albite, Augite, Brazilianite, Halite, Labradorite, Lazurite, Scapolite, Black Tourmaline, and Sodalite

Hydrogen Stones: Antigorite, Apatite, Apophyllite, Azurite, Childrenite, Chrysacolla, Dioptase, Epidote, Lazulite, Lepidolite, Malachite, Opal, Serpentine, Tourmaline, Tourquoise, and Zoisite.

Citrine: Digestive aid; has purgative effect on elimination organs; increases assimilation of food and helps one to reap lessons from life experiences; Promotes manifestation of creative potential. Wear around abdominal area.

Gold Calcite: Reforms thought patterns related to food. Helps create healthier eating habits. Wear in stomach region.

Mental And Emotional Stress

MENTAL

Amethyst: Balances mental functions in brain; sedates and calms nervous system; Opens '1st Eye'; Drains sinuses.

Sugilite: Allows one to think with love, analyze with compassion.

Lepidilite: Natural source of lithium. Balances mind & heart. Alleviates depression and schizophrenic tendencies.

Azurite: Purges mental pollution and imbalanced thoughts that are inconsistent with spiritual principles.

Clear Quartz: In modern urban centers, the melanin of most African-Americans is completely overworked. It is continually processing and filtering a multitude of vibrations and frequencies. When melanin is stressed, particularly the melanin centers of the nervous system, we feel it! Irritability, tiredness, head and body aches, depression, melancholy, and sickness are often the result of the melanin centers shutting down due to being overworked. When melanin centers shut down, internal body messages don't get relayed and the body's organs and systems begin to malfunction.

As a multi-spectrum conductor, clear quartz crystal reduces the workload and relieves stress on the melanin systems of the body by assisting in the assimilation and transformation of vibrations that enter the body. Clear quartz, when held, worn, carried, or laid upon the body, will synergize with the melanin centers, thus realigning and harmonizing them as well. When out of the house, carry or wear clear quartz at all times. When home, recharge and realign by doing crystal bodywork (laying out stones on the body or holding them during quiet time).

Also, Lithium, Phosphorus, Magnesium, and Manganese are elements that are needed for balanced mental function. Crystalline structures that contain these elements tend to strengthen the mind and build mental endurance.

Manganese Stones: Childrenite, Chloritoid, Columbite, Helvite, Manganite, Pyrolusite, Rhodochrosite, Rhodonite, Wolframite

Magnesium Stones: Almandine, Antigorite, Augite, Hypersthene, Idocrase, Lazulite, Magnesite, Olivine, Pyrope, Serpentine, and Talc

Lithium Stones: Elbaite, Lepidolite

Phosphorus Stones: Amblygonite, Apatite, Brazilianite, Childrenite, Lazulite, Monazite, Pyromorphite, and Turquoise

EMOTIONAL

Malachite: Purges emotional baggage and moves out corresponding physical blockage. Malachite is suitable for the whole body, but it is excellent for laying on Solar Plexus in conjunction with clear quartz. Solar plexus region is the emotional dumping ground for the Heart. When the heart experiences emotional trauma, a common response is to suppress the grieving process or improperly ventilate feelings. Our heart and solar plexus thus get filled with unresolved emotional baggage. We then find it hard to feel and share love, as well as maintain order and balance. The malachite will bring tucked away feelings to the surface, and the clear quartz will dissipate them. Have a comforting ear to talk to when going through this process. The result will be an increased capacity to give and receive love, forgive past transgressions, and release the pains of past emotional trauma.

Dioptase: Personally one of my favorite stones, dioptase is beautiful to behold and a very powerful healer. A deep emerald-green stone that has small extensions of semi-translucent terminations, dioptase has the power to send a healing green ray of love DEEP into the heart center. A true comforter, dioptase is a stone of unconditional love. Placed over the heart, one can truly feel the Love enter the body. As its deep green ray enters, it heals past emotional trauma and removes any physical manifestations of that trauma. It's expensive, but well worth it!

Rose Quartz: Invokes Self-forgiveness and self-love; eases heartache; promotes expression of feelings; relieves 'heavy heart'.

Chrysacolla: Being able to express feelings verbally is a challenge for many. Either verbal expression is too excessive and strong, or verbal expression is suppressed. Chrysacolla used over the throat chakra will allow one to express emotions frankly and clearly without being over-emotional and offensive. A feminine-energy stone that looks like the ocean, chrysacolla is good for balancing emotions in general. Chrysacolla is a good stone with which to travel through urban danger-zones.

Carbon, Copper and sulfur tend to have great impact on "feelings", because they are the key elements of melanin; and melanin is the key compound of the sympathetic nervous system. The sympathetic nervous system is the neural connections that coordinate the body's response and reaction to external conditions. Stones with these elements tend to strengthen the sympathetic nervous system, thus empowering one with greater resilience to stressful conditions.

Carbon Stones: Aragonite, Calcite, Carbonite, Carbon Quartz, Smoky Quartz, Diamond, Magnesite, Malachite, Matrix of Herkimer Diamonds, Melanite, Rhodochrosite, and Smithsonite.

Copper Stones: Antlerite, Azurite, Boleite, Bornite, Chalcanthite, Chalcocite, Chalcopyrite, Chrysacolla, Copper, Covellite, Cuprite, Dioptase, Malachite, Tennantite, Tetrahedite, Turquoise,

Sulfur Stones: Cobaltite, Gypsum, Lazurite, Marcasite, Pyrite, and Sulfur

Environmental Pollution

Bloodstone: A green-red jasper that stimulates and harmonizes the liver and other detoxifying organs. Cleans the blood in the process. Lay over abdominal area.

Hematite: Hematite is a stable, metallic compound of iron and oxygen. Hematite means "blood stone", and recognizing that iron and oxygen are the two component elements in blood, it is clear how hematite received its name. When interacting with melanin, sweat, and sunlight, hematite catalyzes the assimilation of iron and oxygen into the blood, thus strengthening the entire physical system. Wear daily.

Pyrite: Iron-sulfate. A 'fire stone' that ignites a purifying heat in the aura. Fortifies personal energy field, thus making it more resistant to toxins in environment. Also cleans and strengthens both blood and melanin. Wear daily.

Chlorine and Potassium are the primary cleansing elements in the chemistry of man. Crystals with these elements tend to detoxify the body of environmental pollutants.

Chlorine Stones: Apatite, Halite, and Sodalite

Potassium Stones: Adularia, Alunite, Apophyllite, Lepidolite, Leucite, Muscovite, Neptunite, Niter, Sanidine, and Sylvite

Innapropriate Use Of Antibiotics And Vaccines

The active agent in vaccines is actually genetic material of viruses. When introduced into the body, they alter the human genetic code. Apply the stones listed under **Genetics** to realign DNA.

Antibiotics tend to pollute the blood and destroy intestinal flora. Combine stones listed under **Environmental Pollution and Diet.**

Dental Factors

Have mercury fillings removed! Then, combine applications for **Environmental Pollution** and **Mental Stress**. Also use:

Blue Quartz: Opens communication center; good for throat, ears, eyes, back of neck, lungs and sinuses. Calms the mind.

Moreover, **calcium** and **fluorine** are vital to healthy teeth. Stones with these elements help fortify dental structure.

Calcium Stones: Apatite, Apophyllite, Aragonite, Calcite, Danburite, Dolomite, Epidote, Flourite, Gypsum, Labradorite, Prehnite, and Zoisite.

Flourine Stones: Cryolite, Flourite, Microlite

Electro-Magnetic Fields

The key to defending oneself from harmful Electro-magnetic radiation is to wear a balance of:

- Ionic stones (stones that generate ions)
- Para-magnetic (stones with EM fields but no magnetic attraction)
- Magnetic stones (stones with EM fields and magnetic attraction).

Ionic stones replace spirit energy that has dissipated as a result of coming into contact with ELF radiation. Quartz crystal is the premier ionic stone. One highly ionic stone in particular is **Double Terminated Quartz Crystal**. This stone is identified by a natural termination at each length. Carrying double terminated quartz is like having an ionic energy shield. It continually fills the aura with an abundance of charged electrons, thus raising the intensity of one's Electro-magnetic field. This is effective immunization from EM devitalization.

Para-magnetic and magnetic stones augment ones' own magnetic field, thus making the bio-magnetic field of the body more resilient when in contact with harmful EMF's.

Magnetic Stones: Lodestone, Magnetite, and Commercial Bio-magnetic products.

Para-Magnetic Stones: Moki Marbles, Boji Stones, Pyrite, Franklinite, Black Garnet, Amber, Hematite, Gibeon (Space Metal).

Geopathic Stress

The same approach for addressing **Electromagnetic Fields** can also be used to address harmful radiation from the Earth.

One may also use naturally radiated stones to help assist one in learning how to live with strong Earth vibrations. Two naturally radiated stones are **Smoky Quartz** and **Kunzite**. These stones were exposed to nuclear radiation during their gestation in the Earth. However, the radiation exposure actually contributes to these stones' beauty and power. Kunzite and Smoky quartz can promote the same response in humanity and assist in the assimilation of unusual Earth radiation. [2]

Tips for Wearing Stones

- Pouches are excellent for carrying stones, for they afford protection. Pouches can be attached to a cord and worn around the neck. The length of the chord can be adjusted so that the pouch hangs at the heart, solar plexus, or navel. Pouches can be carried in pockets as well.

- Cut & polished stones are better suited for pocket stones than natural stones. Uncut, naturally terminated stones often get taxed when carried in pockets. Cut and polished stones make excellent jewelry adornments as well.

- If you wear a headwrap, turban, crown, or hat, crystals can be tucked in to keep light around your head. Amethyst, clear quartz, and Lepidolite are personal favorites for this.

- Flat, cut & polished stones are nice to wear in your shoes. As you walk, they provide excellent foot reflexology massage. Hematite and Adventurine are personal favorites for this.

- Remember to balance your stones. For example, if you choose to carry a strong piece of black tourmaline for protection, balance it with clear quartz, danburite or some other elevating stone. Otherwise, the black tourmaline may ground you out. Depression, melancholy, being overburdened with worldly affairs, constipation, and sleep disruptions are symptoms of over-groundedness. On the flip side, if you decide to carry a piece of phenakite, moldavite tektite, or danburite; at least wear carnelian or hematite to afford some grounding balance. Otherwise you may get lost in space.

- There are only three colors that are safe to wear continuously without counter-indications: Green, Purple, and Orange. In other words, you can carry a stone of these colors as long as you want (months & years) without experiencing imbalances as a result. All other colors produce some form of imbalance if worn continuously for an extended period.

Red - Aggression, restlessness, inflammations, fevers, skin eruptions and boils.

Blue - Melancholy, 'The Blues', poor circulation, cold extremities, impotence.

Yellow - Anxiety, nervousness, heart trouble/palpitations, diarrhea, nervous breakdown.

Pink - Hyper-sensitivity, 'Bleeding Heart', misplaced love, obsessions.

Brown - Low moral standards, corrupt tendencies, inconsistent character, 'shitty' attitude. [3]

Sacred Stones:
The Natural Defense
Against Vibrational Warfare

The city has always been a stamping ground of crime, sin, and debauchery. The Jews identified not only the foreign cities of Babylon and Ninevah, but also their very own Sodom and Gomorah, as wicked. Sybaris, the Greek city in Italy, became a synonym for voluptuousness. It is said of Hannibal (though probably somewhat inaccurately) that by taking winter quarters for his soldiers in the rich and corrupt Italian city of Capua he had depleted the strength of his army. And of ancient Rome it was said that the people flocked there in order to speculate, to debauch, and even to train for a life of crime, and that Rome was the best hiding place for a fugitive from the law. About the end of the nineteenth century the young and already gigantic city of Chicago became the breeding place for gangsterism; London is the proverbial site for murder in all the better cloak-and-dagger stories; the word Paris has almost become a synonym for obscenity... Quote is from "Babylon is Everywhere" by Wolf Schneider, 1960.

There is a silent war being waged against humanity. The battlefield is the mind of every human on this planet. The frontline of the battle is the mind of those humans locked within modern urban culture. The invisible weapons of this metaphysical warfare are negative vibrations, or vibrations that have a destructive influence on life and human culture. These negative vibrations set the tone for the visible afflictions that we see befalling humanity - warfare, political instability, hunger, disease, pestilence, environmental pollution, ecological collapse, violence & bloodshed, addiction, poverty, homelessness, deteriorating family structures, economic collapse & instability, 'ghetto' mentality, gangsterism, etc., etc.

A natural question arises: Who is waging this metaphysical warfare? It is truly difficult to explore this issue without seeming to be deluded by 'conspiracy theories'. However, when one studies the science of sacred stones and understands the influential power the mineral nation has upon the human mind; the name of the group itself reveals who is waging the war and how they are doing it.

The Social Architects

A mason is a craftsman who works with stones. Specifically, he cuts stones into square bricks and erects buildings and other structures with his cut stones. A master mason is an architect, or one who designs buildings, lays out cities, etc.

There are also 'social' groups, or fraternities that call themselves masons. They consider themselves 'social architects', or those who design and layout cultural lifestyle. There are many different orders and ranks of Masons. Many of the orders are simply social organizations. However, there are a few orders that engage in a practice called urban geomancy. Urban geomancy is the ultimate 'craft' of masonry. It involves using stones, buildings, and the layout of cities to create resonant energy fields that empower these few men to have control over the entire social order.

According to Masonic tradition, the 'Craft of Initiated Builders' existed before the Deluge, or Great Flood of Antiquity. It members were employed to build the tower of Babel. The Tower of Babel is a brick building mentioned in the Bible that brought on the wrath of Jah (God) and is responsible for the 'confusion of the tongues'. Genesis, Chapter 11 says:

> And the whole earth was of one language, and of one speech. And it came to pass, as they journeyed from the east, that they found a plain in the land of Shinar; and they dwelt there. And they said one to another, Go to, let us make brick, and burn them thoroughly. And they had brick for stone, and slime had they for mortar. And they said, Go to, let us build us a city and a tower, whose top may reach unto heaven; and let us make us a name, lest we be scattered abroad upon the face of the whole earth. And the Lord said, the People are One, and they have all one language; and this [urban geomancy] they begin to do: and now nothing will be restrained from them, which they have imagined to do. Go to, let us go down, and there confound their language, that they may not understand

one another's speech. So the Lord scattered them abroad from thence upon the face of all the earth: and they left off to build the city. Therefore is the name of it called Babel; because the Lord did there confound the language off all the earth: and from thence did the Lord scatter them abroad upon the face of all the earth....

This biblical passage suggests that when some architects attempted to build a tower and city of brick, the spiritual guardians of humanity felt it necessary to scatter humans throughout the Earth and to confound the languages. This was probably an attempt to quarantine the effects of urban geomancy upon the mind of humanity. [1]

However, it is apparent that 'The Craft' passed down in time. According to Masonic tradition, the next great resurgence of the Craft of Initiated Builders was the Grecian 'Dionysian Architects'. Manly Hall, in his monumental work, *The Secret Teaching of All Ages,* says of the Dionysian Architects:

> The most celebrated of the ancient fraternities of artisans was that of the Dionysian Architects. This organization was composed exclusively of initiates of the Bacchus-Dionysos cult and was peculiarly consecrated to the science of building and the art of decoration. Acclaimed as being the custodians of a secret and sacred knowledge of architectonics, its members were entrusted with the design and erection of public buildings and monuments. The superlative excellence of their handiwork elevated the members of the guild to a position of surpassing dignity; they were regarded as the Master Craftsmen of the Earth. [2]

Hall states that the fraternity spread out to every city on the Mediterranean Sea. When Rome became a power, the Architects found inroads into Central Europe and as far north as England. With them traveled the destructive science of urban geomancy.

What is Geomancy?

Geomancy is a natural science that deals with manipulating electromagnetic and gravitational energies that are received and transmitted at key points on the Earth. *Geo* means 'Earth'; *mancy* means 'prophecy', or 'divination'. The word geomancy implies coming to know the Earth, becoming one with the Earth, harmonizing the Earth. Geomancy involves planting vegetation and erecting stone structures that attract, collect, and project terrestrial and celestial energies into the living environment. Geomancy has also been referred to as 'mystical ecology," earth acupuncture,' and 'astroecology' (Arguelles, 1984). [3]

In most of the original root cultures, geomancy was used to attune humans to the vibrations of the natural order. Geomancy was used to impel members of the culture to live in harmony with creation. By creating harmonious vibrations that would impel people to live in a righteous balance, the King or Queen did not have to compel the people as to how they should live. The ruler would often bestow great land authority to his/her priesthood so they could administer the land with the science of geomancy in mind.

The Khuti (pyramids) and Tekhet (obelisks) of Kush and Kemet; the Mayan, Aztec, and Olmec structures; the pagodas, towers, and mound pyramids of Asia, and the early round towers of Europe were constructed to harmoniously manipulate the electromagnetic (Celestial) and gravitational (terrestrial) energies within the environment. They are literal antennas that broadcast celestial life force. The frequency of this celestial radiation is too high - the wavelengths too short - to be conducted by metal. Metals transmit only the longer wavelengths - microwave, radio, and power frequencies. However, silicon-rich, semi conductive stones such as basalt, sandstone, granite, and limestone conduct short wave frequencies very well. The early agricultural cultures used these stones to erect structures which collected, stored, and projected nourishing celestial energy into their living environment. [4]

Sky Juice

Scientists know that the Earth is in a literal sea of cosmic energy, and that waves of these celestial waters awash the Earth continually. There appears to be three bands of cosmic energy that have significant influence upon the vitality of man, animals, and plants. Those three forms of sky juice are Black Light, Infrared Light, and High frequency microwave radiation.

Black Light is an ionic energy, or moving electrons of very high frequency. This ionic energy is also called ultra-violet radiation. Note that 'ultra' means beyond. Beyond violet radiation is literally 'black light'. Scientists exploring the UV spectrum have identified a small band of Black energy and have labeled it 'eloptic energy' - Electric light. It is the highest frequency of UV radiation, yet also the most subtle. This spectrum of energy seems to promote cell production (mitogenetic), and has been identified as the communication spectrum between plants. In other words, plants emit this energy and exchange information with one another through this black light. Humans emits this energy as well. Concerning urban geomancy, this Black Light shines forth from the apex of geomantric structures. [5]

Infrared means 'below red'. Since red is the lowest color frequency, infrared light is invisible. It is experienced as heat. Peter Thompkins, in *Secrets of the Soil*, says that it is the spectrum of infrared radiation that is most connected with physical processes of the body. He points to the fact that sea organisms thrive deep within the bowels of the Earth near volcanic vents. These animals receive no sunlight. The infrared radiation (heat) of the volcanic vents nourishes these organisms with vitalizing life force energy. Thompkins states that in antiquity, this infrared energy was broadcast through geomantric structures to nourish the soil more so than plants or humans.

> What the monks were doing...was collecting cosmic paramagnetic energy, and focusing it with their round towers onto the Earth in which they planted their crops - 'doping' the plants with that energy. Infrared paramagnetic forces would radiate in waves from the bases of the towers to increase the attracting paramagnetic properties of the surrounding soil, rather than directly affecting plants.... [6]

High frequency *microwave radiation* is the next band of energy that can be conducted by stone. The microwaves that fall from heaven are very high in frequency, yet low in intensity/voltage. These microwaves seem to have a significant impact upon mental functioning, the nervous system, and behavior; for the frequency of nerve impulses within the human body are in the microwave band. Generally speaking, the higher frequencies of microwave energy stimulate mental faculties and excite neural impulses. The celestial sources of high frequency microwave energy are the Sun and other stellar objects.

The three forms of Sky Juice - Black Light, Infrared Light, and Microwave radiation - were the primary celestial energies the priests of antiquity projected into the environment through stone antennas. The structures they created attracted and projected cosmic energy; thus saturating the area with invigorating, nourishing "sky juice." In order for a stone structure to project celestial energies effectively, four characteristics need to be present:

1.   The building must be made of a silicon-rich, semi-
        conductive material;

2.   The building's design must be pyramidal or a tabular
        column (tower) with a pyramidion, cone, or dome apex;

3.   The building must be oriented as precisely as possible to
        the four directions – magnetic North/South/East/West; and

4.   The stone structure needs to be erected over Ley-lines
        (energy lines) or vortex centers of the Earth.

Earth's Embrace

The last two characteristics listed point to the importance of aligning a geomantric building with the energy of the Earth in order for it to be able to broadcast celestial radiation. The celestial energy described is essentially electric in nature. Planet Earth provides the magnetic counter-balance needed for geomantric structures to produce an electromagnetic energy discharge.

The Earth exerts three main forces that are manipulated through the art & science of geomancy: **gravity, magnetism, and paramagnetism**.

In the study of Astrophysics, the law of gravity is considered the dominant force of the Universe. It is a powerful force that causes all things to be attracted to one another. The greater the weight an object has, the stronger its attractive powers will be. Gravity is actually an ultra-magnetic force. 'Ultra' means 'beyond'. An ultra-magnetic force is energy that behaves like a magnet (exerts a force of attraction), but is beyond the frequency of ferrous (iron) generated magnetic fields.

Examples of ancient geomatric structures

Earth's gravity is the force that holds all things on the planet. It is Earth's hug - her loving embrace; her force of attraction she exerts on everything in this realm. The strength of Earth's hug varies from place to place. Generally speaking, the force of gravity is weakest along the equator and strongest at the poles. This is due to the spinning rotation of the planet, which causes centrifugal force to push out strongest at the equator.

However, there also exists what is called gravitational anomalies. These are localized places that have a stronger or weaker gravity field than surrounding areas. Some anomalies occur as gravitational flux, where the strength of the gravity field shifts over time. These anomalies may have either a beneficial or detrimental effect on the environment for humans. The detrimental effects of gravitational anomalies are most commonly experienced as geopathic stress discussed in *Surviving the Toxic Zone*. The ancients used geomancy to balance the gravitational fields and maintain a harmonious gravitational strength in their living environment.

The Earth exerts a rather strong **magnetic field** as well, and actually behaves like a giant bar magnet. Humans are like fish swimming in a sea of the earth's magnetic field, the currents of which flow North/South. This geo-magnetic energy pulses or vibrates at 7.83 Hertz-per-second. Studies indicate that in areas where currents of geo-magnetic energy are intense, people grow stronger and are healthier. Where the Earth's magnetic energy is stifled (concrete jungles of major urban communities, for example), people tend to suffer greater incidences of debilitating disorders. The ancient geomancers manipulated the environment to accumulate an abundance of the Earth's magnetism.

It is interesting to note that research indicates that a giant iron crystal in the center of the Earth is generating the Earth's magnetic energy and magnetic poles. Dr. Ronald E. Cohen, a geophysicist at the Carnegie Institute of Washington, supports the idea that the Earth's inner core is made of iron. The temperature of this core is over 7000 degrees, yet the iron is solid due to intense pressure. These conditions cause the core to crystallize into a single crystal composed of iron atoms. This crystal pulses out magnetic energy waves at 7.83 htz, and is the source of the Earth's magnetic fields and poles. The orientation of this crystal shifts from time to time, causing shifts and reversals of the Earth's magnetic field (Broad, 1995). [7]

'Para' means 'almost'. **Paramagnetism** literally means 'almost magnetic'. Paramagnetic energy is the charged field generated by the molecular activity of certain silicon rich minerals, iron ores, and organic (carbon rich) matter. These substances emit a weak magnetic field, but do not exert external magnetic attraction. In other words, their magnetic field does not exert an active pull on anything. Quartz crystal, sandstone, limestone, basalt, pyrite, franklinite, hematite, Moki marbles, Boji stones, amber, and pearl are examples of paramagnetic materials. Humans with 'animal attraction' and 'personal magnetism' are paramagnetic as well.

Paramagnetic energy circulates around the earth in a gridwork of Ley lines and vortexes. Ley-lines are paramagnetic channels that form a geometric grid around the planet. These lines connect the paramagnetic vortex centers of earth. Vortex centers are circular points on the earth where cosmic radiation spirals down to the planet and accumulates because of an abundance of paramagnetic energy attracting it. These vortex centers are often located where two or more Ley lines intersect. Vortex centers are the high-energy points on the earth. New York City and Upstate New York, Giza in Egypt, Sedona Arizona, Mt. Shasta California, Philadelphia Pennsylvania, and Martha's Vineyard Massachusetts are a few examples of vortex centers. Humans historically settled in high paramagnetic areas - either along Ley lines or on vortex centers. Ancient geomancers often acted as custodians of the vortex centers, treating them as sacred sites, burying ancestral remains there, performing naming ceremonies and healing arts in these regions, etc. It is the flow of paramagnetic energy that determined for the ancient geomancers where to erect a structure.

Vibrational Pesticides

The geomancers of antiquity expounded upon broadcasting cosmic energy into the living environment. The stone structures were used as tools in a technology that is referred to in modern terms as *radionics*. Radionics is a system of vibrational communication. It involves identifying the frequency of a targeted life form and creating vibrations of a matching frequency. The polarity of the vibrations will either enhance the life form or destroy the life form.

This science was intimately connected to the agricultural practices of the ancient root cultures. Radionics was used as a form of vibrational insecticide and herbicide - a process of 'resonant communication' - "a system for affecting life forms by finding and reproducing the exact wavelengths on which it vibrates" (Thompkins, 1989). [8]

For example, if a Kemetic Priest tending the crops wished to eliminate a certain weed or insect, he / she would collect some specimens for a 'witness.' A witness is the 'tuner' which allows the priest to match the frequency of the species. The witness would be incinerated, in accordance with the principle of resonant polarity this principle states that: The Live Vibrations of a species promotes health and fertility of that species. The vibrations of a destroyed species promote death and sterility of that species.

The Kemetic priest would then collect the ash and place it in a central location within the tekhens, Khutis and Djed columns (pyramids and obelisks). The vibration of the dead specimen burned to dust would then emanate throughout the area and have a negative, adverse effect upon the living species. The vibration of the destroyed specimen would:

1. Cut off the flow of nourishing celestial sky juice from the living species remaining in the area.

2. Disintegrate the health, reproductive fertility, and vital form of the species by 'jamming" its own internal frequencies.

The cultures that originated geomancy and radionics were matriarchal, and it was the goddesses, mothers, sisters, and daughters who ultimately dictated how this science was used. Their guiding principles were oneness with nature and fertility of the community. The science of geomancy and the technology of radionics were not abused.

In time, however, a male, patriarchal elite order seized control of the science of geomancy. Their guiding principles for building stone structures were (and still are) to control and exploit nature, as well as enslave the rest of hue-manity. Their first seat of power was Babylon. Their power centers have shifted over time and their cities have risen and fallen, but their mission has been the common historical thread. In contemporary times, the male patriarchal elite is known as Masons, and their centers of power are in Europe and North America.

Urban Geomancy

The Washington Monument is the tallest structure in Washington, D.C., and the central building in this radially designed city.

Philadelphia Skyline. Note the tabular column that resembles a computer chip in the center of the photo. All of the other sky scrapers of simular height have pyramidal apexes.

If geomancy is a natural art and science that deals with balancing cosmic radiation with magnetic energy of the Earth; then Urban Geomancy is a perversion of this science. Urban geomancy involves manipulating the celestial and terrestrial energy in the environment to dull awareness. Modern geomantric cities emit conscious altering vibrations that control the minds, bodies, and spirits of the urban sharecroppers imprisoned within its sphere of influence.

The word urban comes from the Latin word Urbanus, which means 'belonging to a city'. Its roots probably extend back further to the oldest cities in the world: Ur and Urak. These two Babylonian cities, located in modern-day Iraq, were giant city-states before 4000 BCE (6,000 years ago). More than likely, Urak is the city where the mythical Tower of Babel was built. Thus, Urban Geomancy is another name for Babylon City Design.

The process of urban geomancy is as follows: The masons would find a point on the earth that rests on a Ley-line or vortex center. They would then chart celestial cycles from that point to determine the best time to capture the energy of that area of the earth to exploit for their own will. Pennick (1979) in his work, *The Ancient Science of Geomancy*, elaborates further:

> The fixation to a central place of the hitherto free energies of the earth, which were formerly able to wander almost at random, represents the change from the diffuse, worldwide shrine of the Earth Mother to the centralized, geomantically defined temple of the solar god. This changeover was long and drawn out. Coinciding with the beginning of urbanization, it marked the departure of at least part of mankind from direct communion with the earth. By means of this new-found power, the energizing spirit of the place which may usually have visited it perhaps once a year, was made fixed and accessible at all times. Once stabilized, the surroundings were modified in order to enhance the properties of the site, and an ever-increasing complexity of temple was added to utilize it to the utmost... Because of the nature of this power, the time of fixation had to be chosen with the utmost care; any error might bring ill fortune... Being a place of exceptional energy, such a site was a link point between the earthly and celestial. For this reason, the ompholos ['navel' center which marks the fixed point of the energies] was invariably protected

from misuse by being covered with a stone, a shrine, or some other structure which denied access to the uninitiated... (Pennick, 1979). [9]

The ompholos, Greek for 'Naval', is a very important point. It is ground zero - the point where a vortex of spiraling cosmic energy focuses before counter-spiraling into the Earth. It is also where currents of paramagnetic energy are accumulated and discharged by the Earth into the atmosphere.

These captured energies were then tapped to empower the imperialistic will of the elite patriarchs. The Master Masons would establish their seat of power over the fixed point of energy. The seat of power was always housed in a resonant stone structure so they could project their Pale Male Magic out from that point. They would then layout and build a radially designed city, or a city that expanded out from that point. Pennick describes the nature of these cities in Europe.

Centrally organized radial cities expressed the power that emanated from the centre where the military tyrant had his tower or palace. Enclosed and protected from outside forces by a strong defensive system; the central fortress stood as a symbol of temporal power and the immobility of the omphalos about which all else revolved. Centralized cities of this kind emanated from the drawing boards of great architects and planners: such cities were designed by Alberti, Filarete, Martini, Scamozzi and Vasari, among others. They combined the remnants of the medieval Masonic sacred geometry with Renaissance mystical themes and solid military practicality. *This connection between the Masonic arts and military engineering is, despite its seemingly disconnected nature, part of the same tradition. In England from the Reformation, and elsewhere in Europe from the same period until the eighteenth century military engineering was the preserve of a new kind of master mason. His geometrical skills were still merged with a knowledge of the landscape, albeit for a totally different purpose. Henry VXI's master mason, John Rogers, is a perfect example of such a transition from mystical architect to master of fortification... (Pennick, 1979).*

It should be clearly evident that General George Washington, the first President and Mason of this nation, is from this tradition of combining military motives to urban design. The former Capital of the Nation - Philadelphia, PA, and the current Capital - Washington, D.C. are clearly radially designed, with center city being occupied by some form of resonant structures. In Philadelphia is City Hall (the Mayor's Office) and the First Masonic Lodge in the country. In Washington, D.C., the Washington Monument is the central point within the geographical city. It is a giant Tekhet (obelisk), and is the tallest structure in Washington, D.C.

Note that most other major cities in the nation are radially designed and built upon urban geomantic principle just as Philadelphia and Washington. From their central towers of power, the masons broadcast their will power throughout the country. The result is that most people either consciously or unconsciously submit to the will of the social architects. Moreover, the modern urban geomancers have at their disposal a radionic system to bombard any group of people they oppose with vibrations that would disintegrate the health, reproductive fertility, and vitality of that group.

The Military and Modern Urban Geomancy

The combining of Masonic science with military motives is a vital component of modern Urban Geomancy; and as a result the U.S. military is actively conducting vibrational warfare within most cities today. The U.S. Army's vibrational warfare is a component of the 'Psychological Operations' (PSYOP) Program. The Army says that the PSYOP mission is to disseminate the media propaganda needed to justify international warfare in the minds of U.S. citizenry. However, a covert branch of PSYOP uses 'Extra-Low-Frequencies' (ELF) or 'Very-Low-Frequencies,' (VLF) as a form of radionic pesticide against hue-manity.

Today's urban ELF radionic warfare conducted by the Army uses both geomantic stone structures as well as recently invented electromagnetic devises. Vyladimir Valarian, in his massive work, *The Matrix*, describes the frequencies being projected into the cities.

> The use of Very Low Frequency Sound or Ultrasonics has been well documented. VLF sound and Ultrasonics can affect both the electrical behavior within the brain and actual brain tissue. In the current phase of international VLF warfare, pulses of 7-12 Hz are bounced off the 8 Hz ionospheric envelope around the earth. Within these pulses are entrained

bizarre and aberrant patterns that produce equivalent behavior in humans... In 1961, the University of Illinois did experiments on ultrasonic research that eventually got into the hands of the military industrial complex... (Valerian, 1992).

Valerian also identifies the purpose of this "Mind control":

"The purpose of mind control, as far as the United States Government is concerned, is to devise operational techniques to disturb the memory, to discredit people through aberrant behavior, to alter sex patterns, to elicit information, and to create emotional dependence" (Valerian, 1992). [10]

The Army's PSYOP operations appear to be engaged in localized communities in select cities. Usually, these operations occur in the 'ghettos', or poorer communities of urban centers.

However, while the Army is engaged in localized vibrational warfare, the U.S. Air Force is engaged in global vibrational warfare. Through HAARP - 'The High-Frequency Active Auroral Research Program' - The U.S. Air Force is bombarding Earth's ionosphere with intense energy beams.

The ionosphere is a field of free electrons sixty miles above the Earth's surface. The ionosphere is the first band of the atmosphere separating the planet from outer space, and is considered the beginning of the atmosphere. The frequency of the ionosphere is in resonant affinity with the Earth's magnetic field and the Hue-man mind (All three resonate at 7.83 hertz-per-second). This fact reveals the potential threat of mind control by beaming energy into the ionosphere.

The HAARP antennae are located in a remote Alaska outpost. It is a series of radio telescopes geared for broadcasting microwaves instead of receiving them. The Air Force says HAARP is primarily an academic project geared toward studying the ionosphere to improve communication systems.

However, Dr. Nick Begich, in his article "The Very Real Dangers of HAARP", says that the HAARP antennae '...provides the ability to put unprecedented amounts of power in the Earth's atmosphere at strategic locations and to maintain the power injection level, particularly if random pulsing is employed...' . The effects of HAARP are clear: If the ionosphere is greatly disturbed, then the atmosphere below is subsequently disturbed.

Dr. Begich says that injecting powerful microwaves into the ionosphere gives the Air Force the ability to wipe out communication systems, change weather patterns, create 'nuclear-sized' explosions without radiation, create artificial electromagnetic fields, and conduct 'geophysical' warfare (identifying environmental instabilities and catalyzing ecological collapse). If this were not enough, HAARP gives the Air Force unprecedented mind control powers. Dr. Begich quotes an Air Force document:

> The potential applications of artificial electromagnetic fields are wide ranging and can be used in many military and quasi-military situations... Some of these potential uses include dealing with terrorist groups, crowd control, controlling breaches of security at military installations, and antipersonnel techniques in tactical warfare. In all of these cases the EM systems would be used to produce mild to severe physiological disruption or perceptual distortion or disorientation... Another advantage of electromagnetic systems is that they can provide coverage over large areas with a single system. They are silent, and countermeasures to them may be difficult to develop (1996). [11]

More Weapons?

One would think that geomantric towers, ELF generators, and HAARP systems are more than enough weapons for the social architects to wage their war against the mind of hue-manity. However, the social architects have created many more weapons, and have weaved them into the cultural fabric of modern urban culture. These weapons are presented as modern conveniences that make life easier. However, they ultimately create negative vibrations that have a devitalizing influence on life and human culture. These weapons include:

- Televisions
- Microwaves ovens
- ISBN check-out scanners
- Computers
- Unnatural light from fluorescent, halogen, and incandescent bulbs

- Satellite dishes
- Radios and broadcast antennas
- Cellular Phones
- Pagers
- Walkman/ Personal Stereo systems
- Compact Disc (CD) Players
- Appliances with a rotating electric motor (vacuum cleaners, blenders, electric razors, etc.)
- Electric Blankets
- Surveillance cameras
- Electronic pest controls

All of these electronic conveniences emit harmful ELF (extra-low frequency) electromagnetic radiation. The radiation these gadgets emit range in frequency from 30 to 100 cycles-per-second (hertz). ELF radiation is a factor in chronic stress, stunted or deformed cell growth and division, neural-chemical and genetic alterations, immune system dysfunction, altered hormone production and biological cycles, acceleration of tumor growth, and cancer. [12]

Some of these conveniences emit harmful microwave radiation. Recall that the microwaves that fall from the heavens are low-voltage, high frequency microwaves. These microwaves are nourishing and vitalizing to the brain and mind. However, microwave ovens, cellular phones and satellite dishes emit high-voltage, low frequency microwave radiation. This form of microwave radiation has been linked to:

- Devitalization and chronic fatigue syndrome
- Cell damage and decrease in cell mitosis
- Destabilized metabolism
- Brain and nervous system dysfunction
- Hormone imbalance
- Psycho-motor & psychological disorders

Other Effects of Modern Urban Geomancy

To sum up, there are five main types of weaponry being used to produce negative vibrations in the modern metaphysical warfare:

- Geomantric Stone structures. Usually tabular columns (Skyscrapers) with pyramidion, dome, or cone apex. These structures constantly emit conscious dulling vibrations that impel submission to the social architects.

- Radionics, a form of vibrational pesticide. The vibrations are broadcast from center-city stone structures when 'tuned' by the social architects through a 'witness' (vibration of group member that has been destroyed).

- ELF warfare, or the bombardment of certain communities with extra-low frequencies by the U.S. Army. The goal of ELF warfare is to disturb the memory, to discredit people through aberrant behavior, to alter sex patterns, to elicit information, and to create emotional dependence.

- HAARP warfare, in which the U.S. Air Force bombards the ionosphere of the planet with high powered intermittent bursts of microwaves. Many mind control applications exist, including destabilizing vast communities with perception altering vibrations.

- Electronic gadgets that saturate the urban living environments. These gadgets are devitalizing to the mind and body.

Generally speaking, all of these weapons create vibrations that:

- Cut humans off from nourishing celestial radiation, as well as healthy Earth emanations; and

- Jam the internal frequencies of humans, causing mental and physical disintegration.

Some specific ways in which these metaphysical weapons affect humans are:

- Fibroid tumors and cancerous growths appearing on female reproductive organs;

- Young male hue-mans destroying one another (Black on Black violence);

- Degenerated family living;

- Psychotic Behaviors & Self Destructive Tendencies;

- Physical mutilation to change body appearance (processed hair, bleached skin, cosmetic surgery, etc.);

- Sexual misorientation, child molestation, & sexual deviant lifestyle;

- Cultural misorientation - People of Color attempting to appear and act European;

- Disunity and lack of cooperative economics expressed in the community;

- A general lack of awareness within the community;

- Strained male/female relations;

- Disempowerment of the Hue-man within society;

- Prostate challenges in African-American males;

- African-Americans suffering a greater percentage of all health challenges;

- Gangsterism & criminal mindedness in urban communities; and

- Prevalence of poor values, lack of ambition, lack of empowering vision.

Sacred Stones as the Shield against Vibrational Warfare

If you are Human and live in an urban environment, here are some ways to defend yourself from the metaphysical warfare:

- Create a personal ionic shield by continually traveling with one or more double terminated clear quartz crystals. NEVER LEAVE HOME WITHOUT IT! Double terminated clear quartz will elevate your personal rate of vibration, as well as strengthen your own electromagnetic energy field, thus immunizing yourself from devitalizing radiation.

- Create a home ionic shield by placing quartz clusters in the four corners of each room in your home. Place crystals throughout the house, preferably in some geometric gridwork. Pray, play harmonious music, sing and laugh around these stones as much as possible. Make a joyful noise!

- Create a paramagnetic broadcast station in your own home.

Tools needed include:

- Large (at least a 5 pound) Quartz generators or Quartz clusters
- One or more of the following: Lodestone, pyrite, hematite, magnetite, Boji stones, and Moki marbles (the more the better)
- Copper pyramid (details on how to build one are in next chapter)
- Additional copper power tools (Ankhs, crosses, staffs, Genesa crystals, etc.) if available
- A variety of hand-sized quartz generators, preferably double-terminated
- A high-quality stereo system with strong sub-woofer effect.

This is a creative endeavor in which one should allow inner intuition to guide through the process. However, generally speaking, one wants to place the lodestone and paramagnetic iron crystals in a basket. Center the basket within the pyramid so that it is directly under the apex. Place clear quartz at the apex and in each corner of the pyramid. Align the remainder of stones and/or power tools within the pyramid such that symmetry, balance, and order are reflected. Adorn with whatever spiritual symbolism you are inspired to include. Set up the stereo system such that the vibrations from the sub-woofer really resonate strong in the quartz. If you place your hand on the stone while the music is playing, it should vibrate significantly.

Play harmonious inspiring, uplifting, and transcending music as often as possible and as loud as possible. Do not play discordant music or music with questionable morals or values! Bob Marley and conscious Reggae, Gospel, Jazz, Classic Soul, Traditional African rhythms - music that affirms Blackness. Mahalia Jackson, Sun-Ra, John Coltrane, Peter Tosh, Sizzla, Pharaoh Sanders, Doug Cairn, Billie Holiday, Dizzy, Marvin Gaye, Lauryn Hill, Israel Vibration, Norrisman, KRS One, Public Enemy, X-Clan, Poor Righteous Teachers, Stevie Wonder, Miles Davis, Earth, Wind, And Fire, Anthony B, Capleton, Thelonius Monk,

Charlie Parker, James Brown, Curtis Mayfield, Mtume, Oludom, Isley Brothers, Ile Aye, Luciano, Ras Michael & the sons of Negus, Odeon Pope - these are the kind of artists we're talking about! The vibrations of these creative spirits will permeate our homes and community, and reinforce the essence of the Black Self, Family, Community, and Nation.

Familiarize yourself with all domed buildings, obelisks, pyramids, hills, mounds, skyscrapers, Masonic temples, shrines, energy gridworks, etc. of any city you encounter regularly. Find vortex zones where you can channel cleansing ionic vibes into the city's energy gridwork (usually around parks or small bodies of water). Chant cleansing vibes onto the stone resonant structures (**Be Inconspicuous And Careful**). Showering modern cities with ionic vibrations is a form of etheric cleansing, or cleaning the energy field in which we live. Etheric cleansing is probably the most important mission of Africans-in-America right now. As the Rastafari declare, those who fight spiritual wickedness in high and low places must **Chant Down Babylon!**

When a human holds a terminated clear quartz crystal and evokes positive vibes, it has quick and lasting effect on the etheric environment. Hold your quartz and chant Psalms, Prayers, and Positive Vibes. Send Love to the planet and all that live on the planet. Make this a daily routine. Superconduct positive vibes into the ethers as much as possible. Consider your quartz crystal as Earth's microphone. The city is open-stage. It's open-mike time. Step up and chant down Babylon!

Power Wands

An especially powerful etheric cleansing tool is a crystal-copper scepter. One can be easily made. Needed resources are:
- Finger-sized clear quartz points (well terminated and clear)
- ½ inch or ¾ inch copper piping (1 ft to 4 ft in length)
- ½ inch - ¾ inch coupling joint if quartz finger is thick
- A long strip of leather or mudcloth

- Tools such as pliers, pipe-cutters, scissors, super glue, flat head screw driver, etc.

There is no one set way to make scepters. My most powerful wands were created spur-of-the-creative-moment with no forethought or planning. Set the crystals securely in the ends of the piping or coupling, with the terminations sticking out (if crystals are too narrow, wedge in with mudcloth or glue into position; if crystals are too fat, cut slits into copper tube or clip pieces off bottom of quartz). Wrap entire copper tubing with the leather or mud cloth strips in a neat spiral order (it should have the candy-cane effect). Mud cloth can be sewn into a tight-fitting sheath and slipped onto pipe. Adorn with feathers or other personal effects. Fill inner tube with lodestone, magnets, other stones, etc. Creatively substitute stones if you like. Follow your vibe.

This wand, when held by humans, is an **ion beam generator**.

Trod lightly, carry a powerful rod, and chant down Babylon!

The copper-based melanin in one's body will lock into resonant affinity with the copper pipe. The mud cloth or leather will act as an insulator, thus creating a hand-held Leydon Jar; the copper tube will accumulate charged ions particles because a natural insulator will separate two metals -the copper in your melanin and the copper tube -. The crystals at the ends of the tubing will superconduct and send forth ions into the ethers. Charged with positive thoughts, emotions, and lyrical chants, these ions have the power to wipe away negativity from the etheric environment, and purify the planet. Don't abuse this newly found power. What you send forth with your 'magic' wand will surely return.

Right intention is the key!

De-Program and Reprogram

One can use clear quartz and elestial quartz to re-program his/her mind to resist the awareness dulling vibes and shed submissive, disempowering thoughts and habits. Humans are creations of habit. The daily rituals and routines we engage in make us or break us. Many Humans today are caught up in detrimental lifestyles and want to change the way they are living. However, ill habits are hard to shed when living in a Babylon energy field.

Thinking positive, mentally visualizing desired change, and speaking in the affirmative while holding clear quartz is a fruitful way of Self-rehabilitation. Clear quartz and elestial quartz feed back into the mind the positive change that is mentally visualized and verbally affirmed.

The feedback dissolves old thought patterns and re-orders the mind so that new, more positive thinking patterns manifest.

An effective way to perform this is to everyday, hold a palm-sized, well-terminated, clear piece of quartz. Point the termination towards your head or heart, whichever is most comfortable. Visualize your perfect Self manifest without the habits of the past. Say affirmations that reinforce this vision. Some examples are:

'I praise my mind, body, and spirit as a perfect creation of a perfect universe. I radiate total well being.'

'I release my attraction to the substances which enslave my thinking and pollute my body.'

'I know what to think, say, and do at all times and in all places. I am intuitive overstanding. Within me is the wise-mind of the universe.'

'Everything is in divine order. There is nothing to fear.'

'The bad habits of the past have vanished as the mist before the rising Sun. Habits of cleanliness, comfort, and order are now established.'

When creating your own personal affirmations, be mindful to state them in the present and the affirmative. To say, "I will not be afraid of unemployment because the universe will be ever-sustaining," actually calls into existence an anxiety as to whether the future will be as you state it. The present moment, upon which the future rests, is not addressed. Moreover, it states what will not be done (be afraid) as opposed to what is (having confidence). To affirm with power, state: 'I am confident I have gainful employment, for I am in perfect oneness within an ever-sustaining, ever- nurturing universe.

- Avoid the following vibrations; they are weapons in the vibrational warfare as well:
  - Television waves
  - Waves from high tension electromagnetic wires
  - Microwaves from ovens or microwaved food
  - Waves from ISBN check-out scanners
  - Computer vibes

- Unnatural light from fluorescent, halogen, and incandescent
- Satellite dishes
- Radio waves

• Para-magnetic and magnetic stones augment one's own magnetic field, thus making the bio-magnetic field of the body more resilient when in contact with harmful EMFs.

Magnetic Stones: Lodestone, Magnetite, Commercial Bio-magnetic products

Para-Magnetic Stones: Moki Marbles, Boji Stones, Pyrite, Franklinite, Black Garnet, Amber, Hematite, Gibeon (Space Metal)

• Other shielding stones include:

Galena: Fortification! Lead is the densest metal, and Galena, being lead sulfite, makes a dense energy field around the body into which no Babylon confusion can penetrate. Secure and grounding, Galena also increases sensitivity to unseen vibes. A mysterious stone to wear, carry a small piece below the waist.

Black Tourmaline: Grounds out negative vibrations before they can enter personal energy field.

Smoky quartz: Grounds and roots person to earth-plane; promotes security, well being; fearlessness; generosity. Provides protective shield; helps one assimilate UV/Black light and other radiation.

Amber: Amber is an organic stone made of petrified pinesap. It is highly magnetic, and if rubbed, will draw out toxins and foreign particles from the body. Amber is a beautiful stone to wear. When it interacts with sunlight, amber charges melanin and fills the body's aura with a dazzling gold radiance.

'Alas, Alas, that Great City Babylon, that mighty city! For in one hour has thy judgement come.' (Revelation, chap 18)

Bioresonance: Ancient Healing Technique For The New Millinneum

In the previous two chapters, the detrimental effects of certain vibrations (e.g. - geopathic & ELF radiation) were surveyed. However, just as there are vibrations that harm the body, there are vibrations that are healing to the body. These vibrations may be considered *bioresonant*, or energy that is resounding (resonant) with life (bio) force. Vibrations of life force are healing to the human mind-body-spirit. Conducting therapy with life enhancing vibrations is an ancient healing technique of the Nile Valley. Today, Bioresonance is revolutionary-yet-ancient; and it is a valuable healing art for the millinneum shift.

Bioresonance has the promise of:

- Realigning and repairing human genetics;
- Alleviating mental and emotional stress;
- Reversing the debilitating effects of electromagnetic fields and geopathic stress.

Used in conjuction with a detoxification regime; a nutritionally balanced and clean eating program; as well as some form of stress managment, Bioresonance is the key to a healthy transition into the New Millinneum.

Bioresonance involves realigning and repairing the human body at its base crystalline level through the use of magnetic, ionic, and sonic energy. Realigning the basic building blocks of the body through infusing these coordinated energies harmonizes body functions to balanced precision.

Principles of Bioresonance

Recall that the human body is a *bio-crystalline energy system,* a unified group of *bio-crystalline structures that* work together to maintain a balance of life force energy.

The primary *bio-crystalline structure* in the body is the cell.

Cells differentiate to form more complex bio-crystalline structures. They are in order of density.

- Blood
- Tissue (skin, muscle, and organs)
- Bone

A *bio-crystalline structure* is composed of *bio-crystalline molecules* that are arranged in such a way that they conduct life force energy. Each cell contains three forms of bio-crystalline molecules. They are in order of most simple to complex:

- Mineral salts (ionic crystalline minerals)
- Biopolymers (hydrocarbon molecules containing 'many life units' i.e. - amino compounds and melanin)
- DNA (a highly complex biopolymer composed of chains of less complex Biopolymers).

Mineral salts are the crystalline building blocks for *biopolymers;*

Biopolymers are the crystalline building blocks for *DNA;*

DNA is the crystalline building block for *cells;* and

Cells are the crystalline building blocks for blood, bone, and tissue bio-crystalline structures.

So, diseases that manifest in tissue, bone, and blood have foundations on the levels of mineral cell salts, biopolymers, DNA and cells.

Thus, the key to bioresonant rejuvenation is to realign the malignant mineral salts, biopolymers, and DNA of the body through an infusion of harmonically tuned magnetic, ionic, and sonic energy.

The Primary Tools of Bioresonance

There are five primary tools of bioresonant therapy:

- Copper Pyramid Chamber
- Clear Quartz
- Other Sacred Stones
- Harmonious Sound
- Water

In essence, bioresonance involves having a person relax in a bioresonant pyramid chamber, most often laying down upon his/her back. While laying down, quartz crystal and various other stones are placed on and around the recipient. This is called a layout. While in the layout, sacred sounds are reverberated throughout the pyramid chamber. Harmonious sonic energy is what activates the bioresonant energy exchange between the pyramids, stones, and recipient.

The Bioresonant Pyramid Chamber

A bioresonant pyramid chamber is a copper structure of scaled proportion to the Great Pyramid of Giza. A pyramid of such proportions expresses the geometrics of life, and is the geometric expression of harmony, balance, order, and perfection between the spiritual and material worlds. To truly appreciate how a bioresonant pyramid embodies the geometrics of life and resonates these divine qualities, one must be familiar with the nature of geometry and the geometry of nature.

The Nature of Geometry and the Geometry of Nature

Geometry literally means 'to measure the earth.' There are two basic forms of geometry: *Dynamic* and *Static*.

Dynamic Geometry is used to measure movement of light and other radiant energy. This is important because the life-force of the universe is radiant energy. The form-in-motion of spirit is a spiral; and its motion is measured and expressed by dynamic geometry.

The sphere is the most perfect and balanced shape that can be expressed by dynamic geometry. A sphere is a globe in which all points of the surface are equal distance from a central point. All other expressions of dynamic geometry (arcs, discs, circles, curves, ellipses, spirals, cones) are variations of a sphere.

Static geometry is used to measure and express the shape and dimensions of the space within which light and other radiant energy travels. Static geometry is used to measure matter as well. The cube is the most perfect and balanced shape that can be expressed by static geometry. A cube is a solid with six equal square sides. All other static geometric expressions (square, triangle, rectangle, etc.) are variations of a cube (Monteith, 1983).

Dynamic geometry always needs the numbers PI (3.14) and PHI (1.618) to determine and express dynamic relations and proportions. Static geometry does not need PI and PHI to express dimensions and proportions. Thus, PI and PHI have been considered for millennia to be the 'numbers of life.' Structures which have dimensions and proportions that express PI and PHI are imbued with the universal life force (force expressed by dynamic geometry) and resonate life force.

The pyramid is one geometric shape that has the natural capacity to simultaenously express dynamic and static geometric qualities. In fact, a pyramid that has PI and PHI in its dimensions and proportions actually serves as a geometric lens which projects the radiant life-force of the universe (force expressed by dynamic geometrics) into the material realm (space measured by static geometrics).

Pyramids with PI and PHI in its dimensions embody and manifest the state of transformation from a dynamic geometrical state to a static geometrical state. In other words, the process of life itself, in which life-force energy (force of dynamic geometrics) transforms into organic matter (form of static geometry) is embodied in bioresonant pyramids.

Bioresonance means 'to resonate or vibrate with life,' and the life force that resonates within bioresonant pyramid chambers is totally dependent on PI and PHI being expressed in its ratial proportion. [1]

The PI-RA-MID and the "Fire in the Middle'

PI is expressed in the following way:

- Determine the perimeter (p) of the pyramid's square base by adding the length of the four sides (s). The formula is p=4s.

- Assign the perimeter's value to be the circumference (c) of an encompassing circle. The formula is p=c.

- Determine the radius (r) of the circle. The formula is r=c/2(pi). For example, a ten-foot square base pyramid has a perimeter of 40. A corresponding circle is assigned the circumference value of 40. The radius of the circle is 6.36 (40 divided by 6.28).

- Envision the central point of the circle to be the central point of the square base. The height (h) of the pyramid's apex from the central point equals the radius (r) of the circle. The formula is h=r. For example, the height of a pyramid with a 10 foot square base is 6.36 feet.

- The height (h) of the pyramid's apex is to the pyramid's base perimeter (p) as the radius (r) of a circle is to its circumference (c). The correspondance expressed as a formula is: r=c/2pi : h=p/2pi.

Creating this correspondance between a pyramid and a circle is called "squaring the circle" or "cubing the sphere." Since PI is the ratial proportion of a circle's radius to its circumference, this is a way to incorporate PI into the proportions of the pyramid.

As stated, PI is the ratial proportion of a circle's radius (distance from the central point to the surface) to its circumference (length of surface). PI is the constant by which the diameter (the radius times 2) of any circle may be multiplied to get the circumference. It is fascinating to think that this one number is necessary to determine the circular orbit that an electron travels around its molecule, as well as the circular orbit a planet travels around the Sun.

It is more fascinating when it is realized that PI has infinite expression. The decimals of PI continue in a never-ending and non replicative series which is beyond mental comprehension or finite expression - 3.14150817∞. Because of this, PI is considered to be an irrational number, incapable of being the result of rational algebraic equations. PI is also considered a transcendent number that expresses reality beyond material (finite) existence. PI is the numerical expression of infinite creative potential.

The word 'pyramid' means 'fire in the middle' (pyr-mid). The force of PI, the radiant energy of infinite creative potential, is the fire in the middle of PI-RA-MIDS. PI is the key determinant of the pyramid's height, which is measured from the apex to the center of the base. It is here that the force of PI accumulates. Through the geometrics of PI, the fiery, creative spark of the universe is focused into bioresonant chambers.

PHI and the 'Golden Spiral' of Life

Whereas PI is the numerical expression of the infinite potential of life, PHI is the numerical proportion expressed in the organization and patterning of life - 1.618. The numerical law governing the pattern, propagation and organization of life is simple - Every sum is the sum of the two preceeding sums. This is how the pattern is expressed numerically - 0, 1, 1, 2, 3, 5, 8, 13, 21, 34, 55, 89, 144, 233, 377, 610, 987, 1597, 2584, and so on. After the first five numbers in the sequence, the ratial proportion of the numbers approxiamates 1.6180. In other words, 8/5=1.6; 13/8=1.625; 21/13=1.615; 34/21=1.619; 55/34=1.617; 89/55=1.61818 and so on.

This is important because cellular propagation follows this sequence. Cell formation 'spirals' out from parent cells in the preceeding sequence. Therefore, the width-to-length-to-height ratio of cellular growth patterns in nature often express the ratio of 1.6180.

The 'Golden Spiral' is the name Greek philosophers called spirals ordained by PHI. The 'Golden Spiral' of cell propagation defines the structured shapes of many of nature's creations. The horns of rams, the tusks of an elephant, shells of snails, the claws of a lion, the beak of a parrot, all obey the proportions of the golden spiral.

The leaves of many forms of vegetation spiral out from the stem in well defined geometrical patterns which express numbers of the PHI sequence. Willow and rose leaves follow each other by an average angle of 144 degrees. Five leaves will account for 720 degrees, thus completing two 360 degree spiral rotations. Eight cabbage leaves on average create three spiral rotations. Spruce and fir cones have 21 scales on average which will have eight rotations. Pine cones usually have 34 scales and 13 spirals (Walter, 1995). [2]

The golden spiral and PHI sequence may be seen in the Hue-man structure as well. The inner and outer ear, as well as the pattern of hair growth are spiral in nature. Humans have two arms composed of three spiral pivot-joints. The third pivotol joint has five digits. The same may be said of legs. As a whole, humans possess 34 body segments (20 digits, 12 spiral pivots, 1 head, 1 torso).

Moreover, the double helix spiral of human DNA is governed by the proportions of the Golden Spiral as well. The mineral cell salts and biopolymers that compose DNA combine and assemble in such a way that the ratial proportion of a healthy DNA spiral is 1.618. However, toxins, retro-viruses, mal-nutrition, and other stressors alter the DNA spiral, thus changing the ratial proportion from 1.6180. Cell formation thus becomes mal-aligned (malignant), the natural symmetry and harmonic beauty of cell formation becomes distorted, and subsequent cell growth appears as 'cancerous' or 'deformed' growth.

A bioresonant pyramid chamber resonates the frequency of PHI; and through establishing resonant affinity – like vibration - with DNA, re-aligns the 'Golden Spiral' of DNA. Resonant affinity is a state in which there is mutual harmonic correspondence between two things. When a radio is tuned into a station, it is in resonant affinity with the station's broadcast signal. When one pitch fork is sounded and placed near a pitch fork of the same note but of a different octave, because they are the same note (resonant affinity), both tuning forks will sound.

DNA and bioresonant pyramids are overtones of one another. DNA and pyramids have a spiral form energy dynamic and a spiral energy flow. DNA and pyramids both have a 51 degree, 51 minute angle of ascension. The 'Golden Spiral' of bioresonant pyramids strikes harmonic correspondence between the 'Golden Spiral' of DNA structures of the body, thus realigning the DNA to a balanced, proportioned "healthy" state.

PHI is expressed in Bioresonant Pyramids in the following way:

Determine the length of one side (s).

- Divide the length (s) by $\frac{1}{2}$.
- Multiply $\frac{1}{2}$ (s) x the square root of 1.618 (phi). The square root of 1.618 = 1.27.

$\frac{1}{2}$(s) x 1.27 will equal the height of the pyramid. For example, one half of a ten-foot pyramid's side is five feet. 5 feet x 1.27 = 6.3 feet.

This is the same height that one would get if they used PI to solve for the height by squaring the circle. For example, a ten-foot square base pyramid has a perimeter of 40. A corresponding circle is assigned the circumference value of 40. The radius of a circle with a circumference of 40 is 6.36 (40 divided by 6.28 - PI x 2). Therefore,

- 5 x 1.27 = 6.3; and
- 40 / 6.28 = 6.3.

PHI as it is expressed in all bioresonant structures ordains the relationship of the height to the radial width of the structure. The fact that PHI is expressed in both DNA and bioresonant chambers makes DNA and bioresonant pyramids overtones of one another. DNA and pyramids have a spiral form energy dynamic and a spiral energy flow. DNA and pyramids both have a 51-degree, 51-minute angle of ascension. The 'Golden Spiral' of bioresonant pyramids strikes harmonic correspondence between the 'Golden Spiral' of DNA structures of the body, thus realigning the DNA to a balanced, proportioned "healthy" state.

The Pyramid As A Geometric Lens of Universal Life Force

If one takes a plain piece of glass which would normally only diffuse light, and one fashions this glass to have two convex (bulging) sides of certain angles and proportions, one no longer has a normal piece of glass. One has a lens that is able to project, focus, and concentrate light. This concentration of light creates heat and if highly concentrated, fire.

This is a clear analogy to bioresonant pyramids. If one builds a pyramid - the one geometric shape able to express static and dynamic geometric qualities - and one factors in the numbers PI and PHI into the geometric proportions, one no longer has a plain geometric shape. One has a geometric lens which projects, focuses, and concentrates the Universal Life Force of Creation.

Focus, projection, and concentration of this energy has a definite impact on biological functions and organic matter. The ancient Kemites conducted the process of mummification inside bioresonant pyramid chambers because these structures inhibit decay and decomposition of organic matter and induce dehydration.

Peter Thomkins explores this phenomena in-depth in *Secret's of the Great Pyramid.*

Randall Baer, in **The Crystal Connection** (1987) refers to an experiment in which subjects with blood disorders had blood samples taken before and after a thirty minute exposure to a pyramid chamber's harmonic energy field. The experiment revealed that "parameters of the blood that were out of the normal range were brought into the normal range after exposure to pyramid energies. Blood found to be on the high or low side of the normal range tended to be stimulated toward the midranges of harmonization." [3]

Both ancient applications and modern experimentation have demonstrated that the forces of PI and PHI in pyramid structures cause organic matter to reconstitute itself to its original state of order, balance, and perfection.

The Importance of Copper

A bioresonant pyramid made from any natural material (stone or wood, for example) will concentrate and focus Life Force. However, copper is probably the most powerful material with which to craft the chamber. Copper has great ionic potential, and is one of the best electrical conductors of the metal family. Being full of ionic potential, copper pyramids release an abundance of ions into the surrounding environement.

Moreover, copper naturally attracts a magnetic field around itself; in accordance with the law of electromagnetism. This law states that electric (ionic) activity induce a magnetic field and magnetic fields attract electric activity. A copper bioresonant pyramid forms a corresponding geo-magnetic field.

Recall that humans are like fish swimming in a sea of the earth's magnetic field, the currents of which flow North/ South. A copper pyramid chamber that is aligned due North/South will attract and accumulate this geo-magnetic energy, even if erected in an urban environment. It will then discharge its magnetic energy onto anyone who enters the chamber. This magnetic energy is soothing, calming, grounding, and balancing to the human body, and is an excellent compliment to the other forces utilized in the bioresonant process. This energy may be augmented by placing lodestones in a symmetrical grid in and around the pyramid chamber.

Clear Quartz Crystal

The bioresonant pyramid chamber is the first tool with which to conduct the therapy. The second tool is clear quartz crystal. Quartz is used primarily to lay directly on the recipient's body, as well as place around the recipient in a symmetrical grid. Crystals provide three basic functions:

1. Establishes resonant affinity with DNA, thus assisting the pyramid in realigning this biocrystalline molecule;

2. Generate a piezo-electric charge within the pyramid chamber; and

3. Flood the recipient, the chamber, and the surrounding environment with ions.

Resonant Affinity with DNA

In the preceeding section on pyramids, it was established that the 'Golden Spiral' of PHI ordains any organic structure which is spiral in nature or has a spiral form-energy dynamic. The angle of ascent of this 'Golden Spiral' is 51 degrees. DNA and quartz crystal molecules both have a 51 degree, 51 minute angle of ascension. The 'Golden Spiral' of quartz crystal strikes harmonic correspondence between the 'Golden Spiral' of DNA structures of the body, thus realigning the DNA to a balanced, proportioned "healthy" state. Being in a state of resonant affinity with DNA, crystals provide a model of natural perfection for DNA molecules to 'tune' into and realign with.

Quartz Crystal as Generators of Piezo-Electric Energy

Secondly, quartz crystals are generators of piezo-electric energy. 'Piezo' means 'pressure' in Greek, and piezo-electricity means energy created through pressure. This piezo electric frequency from natural quartz crystal harmonizes the internal piezo-electric impulses of humans who are in and around the pyramid chamber.

Piezo-electricity plays essential roles in the human body. Intra-cellular nutrition and assimilation, specialized functions of cells, enzyme activation and suppression, cellular movement and reproduction, and ph control are some of the fundamental biological functions dependent on piezo-electric energy (Cousins, 1986). [4]

Melanin, bone, and mineralized tissue (cartilage, dentin, and teeth) usually generate and maintain piezo-electric energy for the body. Melanin creates piezo-electric energy when pressured by sound waves. Bones and mineralized tissue discharge piezo-electric impulses when pressured by muscular contraction and motion. However, it is these impulses that are disrupted by high-voltage, low-frequency electromagnetic fields common around high-tension electrical wires and other common electrical equipment.

The effects of disrupting these internal frequencies include: chronic stress, mal-aligned cell growth and replication, neurochemical and genetic alterations, changes in biological cycles, immune system dysfunction, and acceleration in the growth rate of tumors and cancers. [5]

The natural frequency of quartz piezo-electric fields of harmonizes the internal piezo-electric impulses of the body and reverses the adverse conditions just cited.

Quartz Crystal as a Producer of Ions

Lastly, clear quartz creates ion particles in the surrounding atmosphere and creates an ionic particle charge within the recipient and the pyramid's geo-magnetic field.

As was established in part one, ions are essential to human vitality. The level of vitality and awareness of humans is directly related to the hydrogen ion level of the blood plasma. High levels of hydrogen ions equate to high levels of vitality and awareness. Low levels of ions in the blood plasma equate to low vitality and awareness. Melanin maintains an ionic particle charge in its role as a low-voltage battery for the body. Music, sound, and rhythmic motion excites ionic-particle circulation. That is why when humans come together in musical celebration, there is always a lot of energy present.

Stress and toxins, however, stifle ionic activity. For example, 'free radicals,' the toxic molecules that rob cells of electrons, steal ions from the physical structure. This sets the stage for a vast array of debilitating conditions; hence the recent trend in 'antioxidants' - compounds that bind with free radicals and remove them from the body. However, even though antioxidants remove free radical toxins from the body, they do not replace lost electrons/ions. This is what bioresonance does.

Ionic balance is vital to people of color. When the melanin ionic battery is charged, humans have energy. When it is drained by toxins and stress, humans have no energy.

Being in a bioresonant pyramid chamber while an ionic particle charge is circulated allows the melanin battery of human's to re-accumulate ions and recharge itself. Also, cells that have lost electrons because of free radicals and other stressors regain ionic balance. This impels harmonic realignment, balance, and homeostasis of the mineral cell salts, biopolymers, DNA, and cells of humans blessed through the bioresonance process.

Types of Clear Quartz Crystal

Clear quartz crystals are just like humans; just as no two people are identical, no two stones are the same. Every quartz is unique onto itself, and has its own energy dynamic. However, just as there are races, families and clans of humans that resemble each other and share similar features, there are families of clear quartz that share similar qualities and common features. The size, shape, number of terminations, as well as the facets and faces of the stone determine the particular family of quartz. Each family has a unique energy to contribute to the bioresonant process. Some forms of quartz that are helpful in bioresonance include:

Elestial Quartz: Angelic beings incarnated in stone.

Ancestral quartz: Quartz that has deep inner-worlds full of spiraling inclusions, apparent chambers, rainbows, and misty wisps. These stones are excellent for making a home for ancestral spirits of the family. Include in bioresonant sessions to establish strong ancestral connection and clear guidance. Also known as Devic Temples.

Auset: Auset (Isis) crystals have a five-sided facet as the largest or most central face. Auset stones invoke nurturance, intuition, motherwit, and obedience.

Channels: The largest face of channel crystals are 7 sided. These stones help one develop clear inner communication and ancestral guidance.

Clusters: Groups of single terminated crystals that emanate from a shared matrix. Small clusters can be laid upon the body. Larger clusters can be used like generators. Good for promoting a communal nature.

Communion Quartz: Quartz that has multiple terminations at one end. It kind of resembles a tight view of the tops of skyscrapers.

Different peaks shooting up at different heights, some thick and central; some small and peripheral. All clearly with a symmetrical apex. These stones help one open up channels of communication with the Angelic beings, as well as with Extra-terrastrials.

Computer Quartz: Also known as 'Lightbraries' these stone look like a cross between communion quartz and elestial quartz. They are clear or milky (unlike elestials, which are usually smoky, gray, rusty gold, or ruddy red.) However, they are etched and layered over most of their body (just like Elestials). They are usually multi-terminated like communion Quartz; most of the time they are double terminated as well. One can use these crystals just like a computer. One can download and uplink information into his/her mind's mental circuitry. One can go 'online', and surf the collective mind of hue-manity. Historically known as 'the Akashic Records', the Collective mind of Hue-manity has memory of every single human experience on the planet. Useful when recipient has plaguing questions or mysteries that are preventing inner-peace.

Double terminated: A crystal that has terminations at both ends. Small ones can be placed on or between the chakras. Large ones can be placed around feet, knees, and head in symmetrical balance. Super-charges body with ions and dissipates stagnant energy. Good for circulation challenges. Place on or around body part with weak circulation.

Elestial Quartz: Elestials are powerful stones. Multi-layered and etched, these semi-transluscent stones have a smoky, rusty, gold, or ruddy tinge running through them. Sometimes Elestials have clear terminations, sometimes the entire stone appears to have facets so that there is no clearly defined termination. Elestial are actually the encoded awareness of celestial beings. The energy of Elestials generally effects the DNA genetic code. It downloads all of the knowledge necessary for ensured survival. A 'side effect' is the realignment of perspective so that one thinks in perfect accord with the divine order of things. The nervous system is reconfigured, and new neural networks are sparked into growth. Excellent stones to incorporate in layouts for people who are in search of purpose in their life.

Encoded crystals: Also known as 'Record Keepers', these crystals have small raised triangles or pyramids on at least one of the termination facets. Usually indicates that the stone has encoded information to download into recipient's DNA.

Generators: Single terminated crystals weighing more than 2lbs. Their massiveness makes them appear as if they generate a lot of energy. They do. Place in and around pyramid chamber.

Kristos Crystal: The facets of a Kristos Crystal alternate in a 7-3-7-3-7-3 pattern. In other words, every other facet is 7 sides (like a Channel quartz) and three sides (like a transmitter) respectively. These stones invoke One Love, Perfect Heart, Universal Citizenship, and a Messianic Mission.

Phantoms: Phantoms have faint outlines of pyramids or apexes within its inner worlds. Phantoms help one go within and get his/her inner world in order.

Rainbow Quartz: Quartz that either has rainbows reflected strongly in its inner world, or quartz that emits a rainbow when exposed to sunlight. The ability to refract a rainbow is actually because of molecular imperfections in the stone due to being subjected to immense pressure. Rainbows help hue-manity express a full spectrum of beauty and accept imperfections in Self and others. Helps one grow stronger and more brilliant after intense periods of personal pressure.

Tabular: A crystal in which 2 of the 6 sides are flat and wide. The shape is similar to a cassette tape or pocket calculator. 'Tabbies' are usually comfortable stones to lay on body. Because there is a lot of surface contact with tabbies, they usually discharge a lot of ionic and piezoelectirc energy into the body.

Time Link: Time links have one or more parallelograms on the sides of the largest facet. These stones connect one to their past & future lives. If the parallelogram is on the left side of the largest face, the time link connects one to past lives. If it is on the right hand side, it connects one with future Self. The past link stone is good to use for anyone who needs to forgive themselves of past transgressions. The future link stone is helpful to those fearful of what the future holds.

Transmitters: The largest facet (or central facet) of transmitters is a 3 sided triangle. Transmitters are good for sending love, healing vibrations, and affirmations to others over distance.

Twins: Twins are two crystals that are joined like Siamese twins. Their terminations are distinct, yet they share the same body. These stones are excellent to help those in need of relationship building.

Wands: A long quartz which resembles a large, straight finger. Good for the therapist to hold while conducting a layout session. Empowers one to direct ionic energy.

Windows: Window quartz have a large diamond as the 7th facet; usually below and in between two central facets. Windows are excellent for those who need Self-assessment, Self-analysis, and personal reflection. [6]

Other Stones

Clear quartz is not the only sacred stone effective in bioresonant therapy. Other sacred stones can be incorporated and applied based on the principles outlined in Part Three. Stones that compliment quartz crystal in a bioresonant session include:

- Copper-based stones, particularly Azurite, Malachite, Dioptase, and Chrysacolla. Azurite nodules can be placed over the first eye chakra. Chrysacolla works well at the throat chakra. Dioptase and malachite are good all over, but especially the heart chakra and solar plexus.

- Striated stones, including tourmaline (all colors), topaz, danburite, and kyanite. Place in between chakras. NOTE: Avoid using black tourmaline above the naval. The lower that it is placed on the body (i.e. coccyx, legs, and feet) the better. Coordinate the different colors of striated stones with corresponding colors of the chakras.

- Magnetic/paramagnetic stones, including lodestone, magnetite, moki marbles, and boji stones. Place in corners of pyramid and around chamber in symmetrical pattern.

The Chakras as Energy Portals of the Body

The stones should not be layed upon the person in a random way. They should be placed on the recipient in a balanced and symmetrical order. Moreover, the color and/or energy of the stone should be corresponded with its matching chakra and placed on or around it.

Chakras are energy vortex centers that run along the center meridian of the body. Each chakra is associated with a mind power, or mind-body manifestation. They are arranged in an octave, or a harmonic of eight. Moreover, each chakra has a corresponding color of the light spectrum. Chakra is an East Indian Sanscrit word that means 'spinning wheel'. They refer to areas where the spectrum of life force energy spirals in and out of the body. There are many of these energy portals spread throughout the body. There are eight primary chakras that run down the length of the spine. Secondary energy portals include the hands, feet, knees, eyes, and ears.

As energy portals for the body, chakras are centers where energy can be transmitted into or circulated around the body. This makes the chakras the focal points for the stones in a bioresonant layout. They are places on the body where the stone's energy will harmonically enter.

Anatomically speaking, within the body at each chakra center is what is called a nerve ganglion. A ganglion is a 'knot' of nerve cells located outside the central nervous system. These ganglia are connected to each other by a neural network, and collectively are known as the Sympathetic Nervous System. There are several ganglia throughout the body; in fact, every organ has a corresponding ganglion. However, the ganglia in the brain and spinal column are the largest - these are the ganglia that correspond to the East Indian concept of Chakras.

Ganglia are highly melaninated centers of the body. In fact, one ganglion in particular is named *substantia nigra ganglion* (the 'very black' ganglia). The high melanin content is what enables ganglia to act as energy portals for the body. As mentioned, melanin has the potential to super-conduct, semi-conduct, conduct, and resonate a wide range of vibrations. Therefore, it is apparent that the highly melaninated nerve ganglion are the physical embodiment of the chakras.

There are two main ganglia in the head – the *Thalamus* and the *Corpus Striatum* – i.e. The Striated Body. The Thalamus is also known as the Cerebral ganglion or the Basal ganglion. These two ganglion process the energy of the Crown chakra and the 1st eye chakra.

Running down the length of the spine are a series of cerebrospinal ganglia, or ganglia that are associated with the cranial and spinal nerves. There is also a series of:

Cervicale ganglion in the throat region (usually 3 – a superior, medium, and inferior); that process energy for Throat chakra.

Thorasic ganglion in the upper torso region (usually 20, or 10 pairs of ganglion on either side of spinal column), which process energy for the Heart Chakra and Solar Plexus.

Sacral ganglion in the lower abdomen and pubic region (usually 8 in total, or four pairs on either side of the spinal column), which process energy for the naval and procreative chakra.

Lastly, the *Impar*, a ganglion in front of the coccyx where the two channels of the sympathetic nervous system unite.

Many traditions hold that the Chakras emanate from the glands of the Endocrine system – the Pituitary, Pineal, Thyroid, Thymus, Pancreas, Spleen, and gonads. This is true as well, for the endocrine system and sympathetic nervous system directly work hand-in-hand in maintaining balanced energy within the body.

However, it is these ganglia of the sympatheitc nervous system that should be the direct target of energy from crystal layouts. In other words, when the layout is done such that the energy of the stones channels directly to these ganglia of the sympathetic nervous system; the melanin within these knots of nerves will be able to transform it into healing energy for the organs and body parts connected to its neural network.

The key to optimizing this energy transference through the chakras / nerve ganglion in layouts is to match the stones and chakras by color. The chakra color scheme is as follows:

Create a symmetrical interplay of stones running down the recipient from head to toe. Powerful healing stones can be placed directly over the chakra, and highlighted by smaller accenting stones. Striated stones placed in between the chakras will facilitate a strong energy flow that will reach the sympathetic ganglia. Large generators and/or phenakite are powerful at the crown. Paramagnetic or magnetic stones at the feet are an excellent counter-balance. (NOTE: Purple and green stones tend to be suitable for all chakras).[8]

Chakra	Body Area	Colors
Crown	Top of head	Transluscent White & Golden tint
1st Eye	Center of forehead	Purple, Azure blue, Violet
Throat Chakra	Neck area	Light Blue & Yellow
Heart Chakra	Chest area	Green, Pink & Gold
Solar Plexus	Center of torso	Green
Naval Chakra	Belly Button	Golden Brown & Orange
Sexual Chakra	Pubic & Groin region	Red
Root Chakra	Coccyx, legs & feet	Black

Fine Tuning Layouts

Tips for a fruitful, healing layout session include:

- Make sure the room where the layout will occur is an uninterrupted space for the entire duration of the session. Turn off the telephone and put up the 'do not disturb' sign.

- Make sure room is clean, especially within the bioresonant chamber. If possible, have fresh air, running water in self-contained fountains, & sunlight in room.

- Use stones that have been cleaned and charged by any & all off the following:

    - Sage 'smudging'

    - Moonlight & sunlight

    - Placed directly on the Earth or in a tree for at least a day

    - Bach Flower Essences & Other Vibrational Elixers (Star of Bethleham & Angelica Flower Essence work well.)

    - Chanting, singing, & sacred sounds

    - Placed in bioresonant pyramid for more than a day

    - Placed on large quartz cluster or large lodestone for more than a day

- Minimize EMF frequencies by turning off and/or unplugging all unnecessary electical appliances in area of the house (e.g. - digital clocks, lights, unplug televisions, etc.).

- Counsel & reason with recipient before session to familiarize Self with issues, challenges, and areas of need recipient has. Make yourself accessible after layout for follow-up reasoning.

- Have recipient do simple stretches before they recline. The neck, back, shoulders, hips, and legs should be loosened. Other forms of stress management (massage, reflexology, reiki, etc.) applied before the layout really facilitates a strong energy flow.

 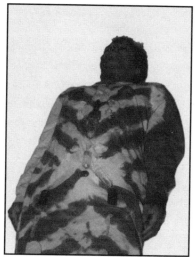

Examples of layouts

- Start at the crown, and progress down the body chakra-by-chakra. Allow wait-time in between applying stones on each chakra so as not to shock the body with too much energy too quickly.

- Encourage recipient to consciously breath deeply.

- Stone-to-skin contact is optimal. If this is not appropriate because of gender or other sensitive issues, use natural fibers such as cotton, hemp, or wool as a cover.

- Be vigilant and constantly observe recipient. Twitching, facial stress, moans, or short rapid breathing may be signs of energy blockages/disruptions. Ask if they are experiencing pain, determine the area, and remove and/or rearrange the stones in that area.

- Once all of the stones are applied, allow them to remain on the body for 30-45 minutes. Remove in the reverse order that they were placed on. Starting at the root chakra, remove stones chakra-by-chakra. Allow wait-time in removing stones.

- Have sacred sounds reverberating throughout the entire bioresonant session.

Activation Through Sound

The last tip is a vital tip; for it is harmonious sound that activates bioresonant therapy. Remember that sound vibrations create piezo-electric activity in quartz. Therefore, it is the sounds utilized that dictate the rhythm, frequency, intensity, complexity, quality, and healing properties of the bioresonant sessions.

Be wise in the selection of the sounds used. Think about what is the intended goal of the session. For example, if the human receiving the therapy wished to expand his or her awareness and acceptance of reality, the music of Sun-Ra, John Coltrane, and similar jazz creators played loudly in sensor-round sound would be powerful.

If the human is trying to wash away past trauma and transgressions, recorded sounds of ocean or spring water playing softly would be cleansing to the soul.

If the human wished to clear and still his or her mind, flute and other wind instruments played around the head would be appropriate. String instruments strum the heart.

Tuning forks of specific notes could be sounded and placed directly on the stones layed over tumorous regions of the body.

Prayers and affirmations could be recited. The key is to be creative and resourceful. There is a sound to harmonize any and all disorders. Use the intuitive faculty of your mind to determine what kinds of sounds are appropriate for the recipient of the therapy.

Sacred Water

Water, the primal liquid crystal of planet earth, is very important to human vitality. A human's body weight is 70% of water. Humans can abstain from food for forty days, but will perish in four days without water. As human perception of health and vitality becomes crystal clear, humans shall recognize the true importance of proper hydration.

Preparation of sacred water.

Sacred water is spring or distilled water that is treated through bioresonance. The ingestion of sacred water greatly enhances and compliments bioresonant therapy. Water is composed of highly absorbant, highly elastic, yet highly stable molecules. When water is treated through bioresonance, it becomes organically structured and highly ionized. Substances that add ions to the body when ingested are called 'electrolytes.' Bioresonant water acts as an electrolyte and aids in the harmonious recrystallization of cell salts and biopolymers.

Summation

In summary, the process of bioresonance involves activating the form energy dynamics of pyramids and crystals through sacred sounds in order to create a harmonic energy field.

- The copper pyramid chamber forms an ionic & geo-magnetic energy field that is in resonant affinity with DNA.
- Clear quartz crystal generates piezo-electric and ionic energies that are in resonant affinity with DNA.
- Sound vibrations activate and set the tone of the bioresonant process.

This harmonious energy field synchronizes crystalline structures within the human body and realigns the bioenergetic patterns within the body to match its original, harmonious vibrational pattern. Water is treated by the same bioresonant process and then ingested. The sacred water aids in the realignment process in subtle-yet-profound ways.

Nutritional Cleansing and Stress Management

Bioresonance is a subtle-yet-profound therapy. As a subtle therapy, it is most effective when used in conjunction with other holistic health practices.

Some form of nutritional cleansing is highly recommended. Nutritional cleansing involves using herbs, tonics, super-foods, and other nutrient-packed food stuffs to: (1) Provide all of the vital minerals and nourishment the body needs to maintain vital healthy functioning. (2) Cleanse the body's blood, organs, lymphatic, digestive, and elimination systems. There is an abundance of literature on this subject available.

As stated, some forms of stress management would complement Bioresonance therapy also. Reflexology, Reiki, Massage, Yoga, other stretching techniques, Aerobic exercise, walking and other heart-pumping-yet-low-stress actions will accelerate the rejuvenation of Bioresonance.

Pyramid Building Tips

There is no one specific way to erect a bioresonant pyramid. As long as the following proportions are adhered to, pyramids will be bioresonantly in-synch.

Start with eight, 10-foot copper pipes, either fi "or fl" diameter (I prefer fi"). Four pipes will create the apex, four will create the base. You will need some pipe cutters to get specific lengths. Buy the cutters that act as a rotating clamp (usually around $7). They are very easy to use. Simply clamp the blade on the pipe by turning the screw handle. Once tight, turn the cutters around the pipe, tightening the blade every so often with the screw handle. In no more than twenty rotations, the pipe should cut clean. The lengths of the sides and slopes are at the end of the chapter.

The easiest way I have discovered is to connect the corners and apex is with pipe connectors. Needed are eight 'T' joints, four '90 degree elbows', and eight '45 degree elbow' connectors. You also need to cut sixteen fittings off of some of the excess pipe, each one measuring 1 inch.

To make the apex, alternate four 'T' joints and four 90 degree elbows by connecting each to one other with eight of the fittings. The result should be a diamond with four slots for holding the ascending pipes.

Create the corners by connecting one 'T' to two 45-degree elbows. Place a fitting in between each. The result should be a 90-degree corner that has slots for two base pipes and one slot for the ascending pipe.

Fit the base and corners together first. The connections can be made tight by pinching the ends of the pipe and fittings with pliers. Then place the ascending pipes into the corner slots. Bring the tops of the ascending pipes together in the center of the pyramid and insert into the slots on the apex.

Reinforce the bond by dropping a drop of Crazy Super Glue in between the elbows and 'T's that make up the corners and apex. Do this only when pyramid is completely and properly constructed. Otherwise, the corners and apex may be set at a wrong angle. Also, do not glue the pipes of the base or ascending slope into the corners or apex if you intend for your pyramid to be mobile or collapsable.

The design of the apex makes it perfect for securely holding a large (3-7 lbs) quartz generator, cluster, or other stone with approxiamately a 3 square inch base.

Be creative, stretch out and apply your own style. Let the construction of the pyramid stretch your creative potential. Create your own corner connections; create your own apex. Be resourceful! However, if you wish to purchase a pyramid chamber instead of building your own, contact *Those Four Sounds,* (web site and PO box are listed at the end of the book.)

Bioreosnant Pyramid Proportions

To make a pyramid smaller than a 7 foot base would make it impracticle as a layout chamber. However, smaller pyramids are effective as room ionizers and paramagnetic broadcast antennae.

Side of Base	Perimeter	Apothem	Height
10'	40'	9' 6"	6' 4"
9'	36'	8' 6.5"	5' 8½"
8'	32'	7' 7"	5' 1½"
7'	28'	6' 8"	4' 6"

Heal the nation with **vibration medication!**

Note to Reader

The information given in this publication is not intented to replace or substitute for medical advice or the services of a competent, legally qualified physician, managed health care provider or hospital. Any person with a condition requiring medical attention should consult with one that is licensed and qualified to treat his or her illness or injury.

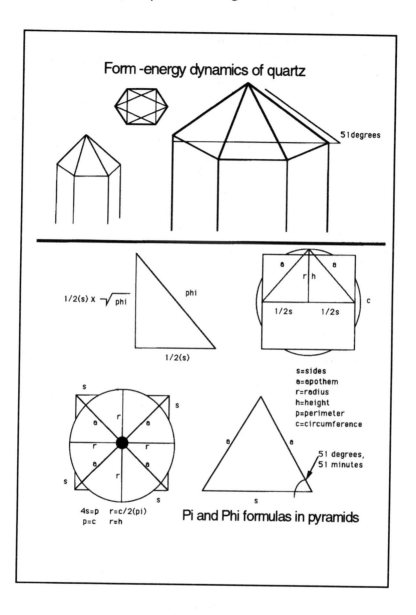

Form -energy dynamics of quartz

51degrees

$1/2(s) \times \sqrt{phi}$

phi

$1/2(s)$

r h

$1/2s$ $1/2s$

c

s=sides
a=apothem
r=radius
h=height
p=perimeter
c=circumference

s

s

r

a a

r r

a a

r

s

s

a a

51 degrees,
51 minutes

s

$4s=p$ $r=c/2(pi)$
$p=c$ $r=h$

Pi and Phi formulas in pyramids

Asase Ye Duru

Asase Ye Duru

Asase Ye Duru means **'The Earth is Heavy'**. Asase Ye Duru embodies the providence and divinity of Mother Earth. Providence means divine intervention and guidance. **Asase Ye Duru says that it is Mother Earth who is the power sustaining and guiding human destiny.**

Mother Earth is a conscious, living, alert, and aware Being. She has thoughts and feelings, and is concerned about her own health, well being, and Self-preservation.

Mother Earth is currently going through profound change. These Earth Changes are a Great Purification in which the Earth Mother is ridding herself of inharmonious cultures that are growing like cancerous tumors on her beautiful body. Earthly children of all sorts die and suffer in these metropolitan lesions. Toxins spew into the surrounding Earth from these viral-like cultures. Spores of humankind advance forth from these concrete jungles and attack the vital points of the Earth, stealing her sacred oils, metals, crystals, and stones. They bore deep into the Earth, strip the surface of the Earth, pump, drill and suck out of the Earth. After they use these vital resources of the Earth, they return the toxic by-products back into the land, sea, and air, polluting and corrupting this beautiful planet. Asase Ye Duru says this must stop!

Asase Ye Duru says that every single human on planet Earth has a conscious decision to make: On which side of the Great Purification are you going to be? Are you going to be one who gets destroyed by a catastrophic Earth change because you continued to destroy the natural world and oppress natural people? Asase Ye Duru says that earthquake, brimstone & fire, tidal wave, lava, lightening, thunderstorm, hurricane, tornado, solar flares, flood, and drought, are coming! The Earth is Heavy.

Asase Ye Duru asks 'Are you going to align yourself with the Earth and help her in her effort of establishing truth, justice, righteousness, balance, harmony, love, and divine order?' Asase Ye Duru says that crystals and sacred stones are divine extensions of the Earth Mother. They are a part of her, and the human custodian of a sacred stone is helping mother Earth balance her energy and heal herself. Asase Ye Duru says that there is no better way to align yourself with the Earth Mother than through working with crystals, gems, and sacred treasures of the Earth. Do not attempt to hoard and covet sacred stones. Be their custodians and guardians, facilitate them and their efforts of balancing humanity and the planet.

Asase Ye Duru says that righteous custodianship of sacred stones is a way of empowering oneself to survive the Great Purification. *The Rocks of Ages* are the firm foundation upon which to stand through this perilous time. Asase Ye Duru says that by using sacred stones to survive the Great Purification of Mother Earth, humanity will learn the keys to creating a powerful spiritual technology for the new millennium. *Asase Ye Duru - The Earth is Heavy*.

The Prophecy of the White Stone

He who has an ear, let them hear what the spirit says onto the churches: To him that overcomes will I give to eat of the hidden manna, and I will give him a white stone, and in the stone there will be a new name written, which no man knows except he who receives it. Revelation, chap. 2

The Lord's Everlasting Love for Israel

O thou who are afflicted, tossed with storm winds and not comforted, behold I will lay for thee stones of beautiful colors, and lay thy foundations with sapphires. I will make thy windows of agate, thy gates shall be of carbuncle, and thy walls of pleasant crystal. And all of thy children shall be taught of the Most High Jah Ra Star For I and great shall be the peace of thy children. They shall be established in Maat, they shall live far from oppression, fear, and terror; it shall come not near them... Isaiah, chap. 54

The New Jerusalem

...[One of the Seven Angels] carried me away in the spirit to a great and high mountain, and showed me that great city, the holy Jerusalem, descending out of heaven from God and having the Glory of God: and her light was like unto a stone most precious, even like a jasper stone, clear as crystal; and the city had a wall high and great, and had twelve gates and at the gates twelve angels... And the building of the wall was of jasper: and the city was pure gold, like onto clear glass. And the foundations of the wall of the city were garnished with all manner of precious stones. The first foundation was jasper; the second sapphire; the third, a chalcedony; the fourth, an emerald; the fifth sardonyx; the sixth sardius; the seventh, chrysolite; the eighth, beryl; the ninth a topaz; the tenth, a chrysoprasus; the eleventh, a jacinth; the twelfth, an amethyst. And the twelve gates were twelve pearls; every gate was of one pearl: and the street of the city was pure gold, as it were transparent glass. And I saw no temple therein; for the Lord God Almighty Ra Star For I and the Lamb Iyahsus Kristos are the temple of it... Revelation, chap 21.

GIVE THANKS

I give thanks to the Most High Creator, the source of Word, Sound-Power and Inspiration for giving I the Creative Spirit to make this works manifest;

I give thanks to the ancestors, both known and unknown, for trodding the road of life with I.

I give thanks to my family, the Hopson clan, the Turner clan, the Pair clan, the Cook clan, the Williams clan. When it is all said and done, all we have is ourselves. I love you all unconditionally and without apology!

I give thanks to the cultural community of Washington, DC for the love and support given towards our efforts of bringing this information to the people. Special thanks to the following for the Cooperative Economics: Brother Bey & 'Da Place' of Healing and Happiness; Grace & Gerald Venerable of Entre Noir; Duku, Kweku & the Blue Nile Family; Ras Tamerot & Mama Jahwey; Ras Ibeju & Mama Adwa; Ras Nefta & Empress Nyabinghi; Ras Mugabe & Mama Moona; Harper Dread and Ras Alimayhu. I love you all unconditionally and without apology!

I give thanks to the cultural community of Philadelphia, PA for the love and support given towards our efforts of bringing this information to the people. Special thanks to the following for the Cooperative Economics: Nisa-Ra and the Bird of Paradise Family; Imah Jordan, Zion Lion, & Kunjite; Nana Korantemaa and the Asona Aberade Shrine; Kemba Nature & Family; the Dandelion Bunch; Bro. Kofi & Sister Altha; Abu and Aya; Mwata & the Merchants of Alkebulan Family; Ron Wandering Feather; Kesiwa & family; Erlene Green & Inertia; Sister Khummit; Brother Hussein Allusawe; Dr. Monica Gaskins & Glenda Gracia; Sisters Marcy, Fatima Bey, & Joan Royal Taylor; David Bey & family; Gerald & Sesmhi; El Ha Gahn; Landis Rowe ('Uncle Shakara') & family; Christine Wiggins & the Imhotep Institute family; Baba Kamau Kenyatta; Sitti Rahman & family. Ras Rodney and Mama Tina. I love you all unconditionally and without apology!

Endnotes and Sources

Vibes from the Scribe...

In citing the sources for this work, I must acknowledge that the ultimate source of this material is the Most-High Creator of the Universe who has revealed himself to this humble scribe in the personality of His Imperial Majesty Emperor Haile Selassie. Kings of Kings, Lord of Lords, Conquering Lion of the Tribe of Judah, Elect of Jah and the Light of this World. Christ in his Kingly Character, the Strength and Redeemer of the world. Jah Rastafari's love and inspiration is the source of the *Rocks of Ages.*

This information was communed to I-man over a seven-year period, during which time I was facilitating workshops and healing sessions with sacred stones. I know that for me to say this information was communed and revealed through inner-communication would cause many to question the credibility of the work. Therefore, I made a serious effort to 'ground' the information communed in verifiable research. When the Great Spirit would whisper the information in my inner-ear, I would write it down and then research what was revealed. In doing this, I attempted to make sure the information presented is as accurate and truthful as possible. I encourage the reader to critically examine the information presented and to check the sources cited. My ultimate goal is that Ma'at – Truth, Justice, Righteous, Love, Harmony, Righteousness, and Divine Order – is reestablished on planet Earth. If there is anything presented that would prevent the Truth of Ma'at from standing firm, I welcome correction. Love and Ra-spect to all – Rastafari!

Part One: Akoben

[1]Hertz: Hertz is a measurement or unit of frequency that was formulated by a physicist named Heinrich Hertz around the turn of the century. A hertz is equal to one wavelength cycle per second. In other words, how long does it take the photon to make one complete wave motion. Therefore, when frequencies are measured in hertz, one is measuring how many wave patterns that photon would make in one second. For example, optical light's frequency begins around 10^{15} hertz. That means that the radiant photon that makes up the light makes 1,000,000,000,000,000 wave patterns in one second. Power frequencies begin around 10^4 hertz. That means that the traveling electrons in power frequencies make 10,000 wave patterns per second.

Source:

Williams, Trinklein and Metcalfe (1984). **Modern Physics.** Holt, Rinehart, and Winston Publishers, USA.

[2]Super-conductivity: Super-conductivity is the ability of matter to transmit energy without providing any impedance or resistance to the energy. The matter must also be able to maintain stability and order; it cannot breakdown while super-conducting the energy. Western scientist consider superconductivity to be a condition that can only be created by freezing certain metals to extreme temperatures (around –600 degrees Fahrenheit). In these conditions, metals such as titanium, aluminum, tin, and lead can super conduct power frequencies and remain stable. The extreme temperatures needed have prevented modern scientist from making sustainable super conductors of power frequencies. However, there are many forms of matter that can super-conduct the higher frequencies of the Electro-magnetic spectrum at room temperature. Two multi-spectrum super-conductors of note are melanin and quartz crystal.

Sources:

Baer, Randall and Vicki. (1987) **The Crystal Connection: A Guidebook for Personal and Planetary Ascension.** San Francisco: Harper & Row Pub.

Barnes, Carol. (1988) **Melanin: Chemical Key to Black Greatness.** Texas: Black Greatness Series.

Williams, Trinklein and Metcalfe (1984). **Modern Physics.** Holt, Rinehart, and Winston Publishers, USA.

[3]Cousins, Gabriel. (1986) **Spiritual Nutrition and the Rainbow Diet.** California: Cassandra Press.

[4]Baer, Randall and Vicki. (1987) **The Crystal Connection: A Guidebook for Personal and Planetary Ascension.** San Francisco: Harper & Row Pub.

[5]The primary sources for information on melanin that were referenced are:

Barnes, Carol. (1988) **Melanin: Chemical Key to Black Greatness.** Texas: Black Greatness Series.

Pookrum, Jewel, (1992) **Vitamins and Minerals From A to Z.** Michigan: J.E.W.E.L. Publications.

Dorland's Illustrated Medical Dictionary. 24th Ed. (1965) W.B. Saunders Co., USA.

Jenson, Bernard (1983) **The Chemistry of Man.** California: Bernard Jenson International .

Part Two: Sankofa

[1]Herodotus. (1942 Reprint) **The Persian Wars.** New York:Random House.

[2]Ibid, p.222.

[3]An African-oriented survey of Pliny's Natural Histories can be found in: **Africa & Africans as Seen by Classical Writers: The William Leo Hansberry African History Notebook,** Volume Two. Edited by Joseph Harris. (1982) Washington, DC: Howard University Press.

Plato's entire account of the Atlantis legend is recounted in **Atlantis: The Antediluvian World** by Ignatius Donnelly (1831-1901). Rudolf Steiner and Harper & Row Publishers (San Francisco) published a 1971 reprint.

[4]Massey, Gerald (1988 Reprint): **Ancient Egypt: Light of the World.** California: Health Research, Inc.

[5]Budge, Wallace. (1967 Reprint): **Egyptian Book of the Dead:** New York: Dover Pub.

[6]These archeological anomalies are explored in **Serpent in the Sky: The High Wisdom of Ancient Egypt** by John Anthony West (1989). New York: The Julian Press.

[7]Two sources for exploring the myths and legends of ancient Atlantis are: Caldecott, Moyra (1990): **Crystal Legends.** Great Britain, The Aquarian Press.

Cayce, Edgar, (1968): **Edgar Cayce on Atlantis.** New York, Paperback Library, Inc.

[8]Smith, Michael, (1990): **Crystal Power.** Minnesota, Llewellyn Publications. This is a powerful book that explores Atlantean crystal technologies.

[9]Budge, Wallace. (1967 Reprint): **Egyptian Book of the Dead:** New York: Dover Pub.

[10]Budge, Wallace, (1987 reprint of 1893 original). **The Mummy: A Handbook of Egyptian Funerary Archeology.** London: KPI Paperbacks. P.266.

[11]A survey of the initiation rites of The Ritual may be found in: Massey, Gerald (1988 reprint) **Ancient Egypt: Light of the World,** California: Health Research, Inc.

[12]Diop, Cheikh Anta (1983). **Pigmentation of the Ancient Egyptians: Test by Melanin Analysis.** "Bulletin de L'institut fondamental D'Afrique Noire", Serie B, Sciences Humaines, Tome XXXV, No. 3 Juillet, 515-530. This research is also referenced in Diop, Chiekh Anta. (1986) *"Origins of the Ancient Egyptians."* Article in **Great African Thinkers: Chiekh Anto Diop.** Ivan Van Sertima, edit. New Jersey: Transaction Books.

[13]Amen, Nur Ankh (1993), **The Ankh: African Origins of Electromagnetism** New York: Nur Ankh Amen Press.

[14]For powerful information on the ancient Judaic World, explore: Godbey, Allen (1974 reprint of 1930 original). **The Lost Tribes A Myth: Suggestions Towards Rewriting Hebrew History.** New York: KTAV Publishing House.

Williams, Joseph (1967 reprint of 1930 original). **Hebrewisms of West Africa: From Nile to Niger with the Jews.** New York: Biblo and Tannen.

[15]Finegan, Jack (1946) **Light From the Ancient Past: The Archeological Background of the Hebrew-Christian Religion.** New Jersey: Princeton University Press.

[16]Ibid, p. 44.

[17]Ibid, p. 49.

[18]A survey of the descriptions of the Ibri within Sumarian texts can be found in: Stitchin, Zecharia. (1985) **Wars of Gods and Men.** New York: Avon Press.

[19]A comprehensive, African-Centered review of Sumarian culture and the incursions of the Mar-Tu into the Black-Headed People's land may be found in a series of articles written by Runoko Rashidi. These articles are published in:

The African Presence in Early Asia (1988): Ivan Van Sertima and Runoko Rashidi Editors. New Jersey: Transaction Books. The quote concerning the Mar-Tu is on p.19.

[20]Apion's writing have not survived history intact, but a glimpse into Apion' perspective on the racial identity of Ancient Israel may be gained from Flavius Josephus' work 'Flavius Josephus Against Apion'. It should really be titled: 'Flavius Josephus Against Apion and Manetho', because the thrust of his argument is to disapprove what both of these ancient historians argued: that Moses was a priest from Heliopolis (Anu) who was in conflict with 'polluted' Egyptians who had a power base at Avaris (Het-Uart).

Flavius Josephus was a literal Louis 'Skip' Gates of the 1st century used by the Roman Empire to spread misinformation to the Mediterranean world concerning the ethnic origins of the Hebrew Israelites. He was a Pharisee, the traitor priests of Judah who co-opted and cooperated with the successive waves of foreign dominators – the Babylonians, Persians (Assyrians), Greeks, and Romans. A revolt occurred in Judah in 66 CE that resulted in the mass suicide of the rebels. Josephus, however, surrendered to the Romans and was taken as a prisoner of war. He gained favor with the Roman emperor Vespasian and settled in Rome as a citizen. While a sell-out Roman citizen, he wrote *Antiquities of the Jews, the Jewish War,* and an autobiography.

As stated in the text, Apion was a dispersed Israelite who lived in Kemet during the Greek (Ptolemy) occupation of the Nile Valley. He argued that Israel was originally Kemetic, and that Israel 'swore by God, the Maker of Heaven and Earth and Sea to bear no good will to any foreigner, and particularly to none of the Greeks'.

[21]Manetho was a Kemetic priest-scholar who lived between 300-200 BCE. He recorded Kemetic history for the Greek Ptolemy rulers. Manetho's works have not survived history intact and have been lost

like Apion's (I doubt it is coincidental that Manetho's and Apion's historical accounts were 'lost', yet Flavius Josephus' survived). However, his list of Kemetic Kings were recorded by other ancient writers and thus preserved. In arguing against Manetho's perspective of who the biblical Moses was, Flavius Josephus preserved a glimpse of Manetho's stance on the issue. These are Josephus' quotes of Manetho:

There was a king of ours whose name was Timaus. Under him it came to pass, I know not how, that God was averse to us, and there came, after a surprising manner, men of ignoble birth out of the eastern parts, and had boldness enough to make an expedition into our country, and with ease subdued it by force, yet without our hazardsing a battle with them. So when they had gotten those that governed us under their power, they afterwards burnt down our cities, and demolished the temples of the gods, and used all the inhabitants after a most barbarous manner; nay, some they slew, and led their children and their wives into slavery. At length they made one of themselves king, whose name was Salatis... and he found in the Saite nomos (Sethroite) a city very proper for this purpose, and which lay upon the Bubastic channel, but with regard to a certain notion was called Avaris, this he rebuilt, and made very strong by the walls he built about it....These people, whom we have before named kings, and called shepherds [Hyk-sos, or 'Shepherd Kings'] also, kept possession of Egypt five hundred and eleven years...[then] the kings of Thebais and the other parts of Egypt made an insurrection against the Shepherds, and that a terrible and long war was made between them...That under a king, whose name was Alisphragmutthosis [Ahmose I, the biblical Moses], the Shepherds were subdued by him and were indeed driven out of other parts of Egypt....

Flavius Josephus Against Apion may be found in:

Josephus, Flavius. **The Life and Works of Flavius Josephus**. Translated by William Whiston (1948). Philadelphia: John C. Winston Co.

[22]Tacitus was a Roman scholar who lived from about 44 to 120 CE. He wrote two works, *Histories, and Annals*. Tacitus was opposed to the imperialistic form of government in Rome during his time.

[23]Celcus is an obscure Roman author. More on the 'well informed Roman' can be found in:

Massey, Gerald (1988 reprint) *Ancient Egypt: Light of the World*, California: Health Research, Inc.

[24]Polemos a first century Roman historian who wrote a work entitled Egyptian Histories. More information on Polemo can be found in:

Massey, Gerald (1988 reprint) **Ancient Egypt: Light of the World**, California: Health Research, Inc.

[25]Diodorus Siculus ('The Gift of God from Sicily') was a historian who lived around 80-20 BCE. In his work, He documented the clearest, extant evidence that ancient Egypt was an African civilization. He quotes the Ethiopian priests he encountered in Kemet as saying:

> The Ethiopians say that the Egyptians are one of their colonies which was brought into Egypt by Osiris. They even allege that this country was originally under water, but that the Nile, dragging much mud as it flowed from Ethiopia, had finally filled it in and made it a part of the continent...They add that from them, as from their authors and ancestors, the Egyptians get most of their laws. It is from them that the Egyptians have learned to honor kings as gods and bury them with such pomp; sculpture and writing were invented by the Ethiopians...

Source:

Diop, Chiehk Anta (1974) African Origin of Civlization: Myth or **Reality.** Conneticut: Lawrence Hill & Company.

The reference to Diodorus's description of the Amen-Ra priesthood at Napata is found in:

Budge, Wallace, (1987 reprint of 1893 original). **The Mummy: A Handbook of Egyptian Funerary Archeology.** London: KPI Paperbacks.

[26]Wallace Budge's comment on the popularity of Set after the Setian priesthood collaborated with the nomadic invaders may be found in:

Budge, Wallace, (1987 reprint of 1893 original). **The Mummy: A Handbook of Egyptian Funerary Archeology.** London: KPI Paperbacks.

Manetho's identification of the Setians with the oppressive Pharoahs of Avaris may be found in:

Flavius Josephus Against Apion: Josephus, Flavius. **The Life and Works of Flavius Josephus.** Translated by William Whiston (1948). Philadelphia: John C. Winston Co.

[27]**The Holy Bible. King James Version:** The Open Bible Edition. Tennessee: Royal Publishers. The quote may be found in Exodus (ch.1).

[28]Ibid. **The Book of Jasher** is mentioned in Joshua (ch. 10) and II Samuel (ch. 1).

[29]**Josephus, Flavius. The Life and Works of Flavius Josephus.** Translated by William Whiston (1948). Philadelphia: John C. Winston Co.

[30]If Ahmose I is the Biblical Moses, then Kikianus is the Greek name of Kamose, the Napatan/Theban general who was waging unsuccessful campaigns against the Eastern nomads who had settled in and around the Nile Valley. Kamose died in battle attempting to expel nomadic Setian invaders. Once Kamose passed, Ahmose assumed the throne and founded the 18th dynasty, married Nefartari the beautiful Ethiopian princess, and continued the efforts of Kamose.

[31]**The Book of Jasher** (1966 reprint of 1840 original) New York: M.M. Noah & A.S. Gould Publishers. The account of Moses reigning over Kush can be found in Chapters LXXII-LXXIII.

[32]The science of the Ark as a Leyden jar is explored in the powerful book: Amen, Nur Ankh (1993). **The Ankh: African Origins of Electromagnetism,** New York: Nur Ankh amen Press.

33Hancock, Graham (1992) **The Sign and the Seal.** New York: Crown Pub. He says plainly: "…some of the most serious biblical scholarship that I studied argued that the Tablets of Stone contained within the Ark of the Covenant had, in reality, been two pieces of a meteorite". (p.67)

34Wilkinson Gardner, (1853) **The Ancient Egyptians: Their Life and Customs.** New York: Crescent Books. References to Ark-shrines can be found on p.267-270.

35The Shamir stone, Solomon and the Shedd King is chronicled in **The Talmud,** the mass collection of Judaic 'research' and folklore. This mythic drama is also explored in: Hall, Manley. (1907) **Secret Teachings of All Ages.** California: Philosophical Research Society, P. LXXVII.

36Budge, E.A. Wallace **The Queen of Sheba and her Only Son Menylek** (London, 1922). The description of the contents of the Ark can be found in Chapter 17, 'Concerning the Glory of Zion'.

37Berhene Meskel Zelelew was interviewed by Graham Hancock in: **The Sign and the Seal.** (1992) New York: Crown Pub. P.15-21.

38Ibid, 194-197.

39Budge, E.A. Wallace **The Queen of Sheba and her Only Son Menylek** (London, 1922). The description of the *mak'das* can be found in Chapter 17, 'Concerning the Glory of Zion'.

40**The Book of Enoch.** Translated by R.H. Charles (1917) London: Holy Trinity Church. *The Home of the Ancient of Days* is described in chapter 14. *The Paths of Angels* is found in Chapter 18.

41Cowan, James. (1989) *Mysteries of the Dreamtime.* Australia: Prism Unity Co.

42Dogon cosmology is presented in-depth in: Griaule, Marcel and Germaine Dieterlen. (1986) **The Pale Fox.** Arizona: Continuum Foundation.

Ogotemmeli's description of the dougue stones is in: Griaule, Marcel and Germaine Dieterlen (1965) **Conversations with Ogotemmeli.** London: Oxford University Press. P. 50-53.

[43]Butt-Thompson, Capt. F.W. (1969) **West African Secret Societies.** New York: Argosy Antiquarian, LTD.

Part Three: Aya

Principles for Overstanding the Properties of the Mineral Nation

[1]The primary sources for mineral properties, stones they are found in, as well as functions in the body are: Arem, Joel (1973) **Rocks and Minerals.** Arizona: Geoscience Press, Inc.

Jenson, Bernard (1983) **The Chemistry of Man.** California: Bernard Jenson International .

Pookrum, Jewel, (1992) **Vitamins and Minerals From A to Z.** Michigan: J.E.W.E.L. Publications.

[2]Arem, Joel (1973) **Rocks and Minerals.** Arizona: Geoscience Press, Inc.

Williams, Trinklein and Metcalfe (1984). **Modern Physics.** Holt, Rinehart, and Winston Publishers, USA.

Metcalfe, Williams, and Castka (1982). **Modern Chemistry.** Holt, Rinehart, and Winston Publishers, USA.

[3]Arem, Joel (1973) **Rocks and Minerals.** Arizona: Geoscience Press, Inc.

Principles for the Synergy of Melanin and Sacred Stones

[1]The primary sources for information on melanin that were referenced are: Barnes, Carol. (1988) **Melanin: Chemical Key to Black Greatness.** Texas: Black Greatness Series.

Pookrum, Jewel, (1992) **Vitamins and Minerals From A to Z.** Michigan: J.E.W.E.L. Publications.

Dorland's Illustrated Medical Dictionary. 24th Ed. (1965) W.B. Saunders Co.,

Jenson, Bernard (1983) **The Chemistry of Man.** California: Bernard Jenson International.

NTU

[1]Nobles, W.W. (1972) African Philosphy: Foundations for Black Psychology. In R. Jones (Ed.) **Black Psychology** (1st ed.) New York: Harper & Row

Myers, Linda (1988) **Understanding an Afrocentric world view: Introduction to an optimal Psychology.** Dubuque, Iowa: Kendall/Hunt Publishing Co.

Akbar, Niam (1985) **Nile Valley Origins of the Science of the Mind.** In Van Sertima (Ed.) Nile Valley Civilizations. New Jersey: Rutger University Africana Studies Pub.

Baldwin, James (1976) **Black Psychology and Black Personality.** Black Books Bulletin Vol 4, Issue 3. P. 6-11, 65.

[2]Nobles, W.W., Goddard L. & Cavill, W III (1985) **The KM EBIT** Husia California: Institute for the Advanced Study of Black Family Life and Culture.

Azibo, DA **Liberation Psychology** (1992) Unpublished Manuscript presented at Temple University Department of African American Studies.

[3]Phillips, Frederick B. (1990) **NTU Psychotherapy: An Afrocentric Approach.** The Journal of Black Psychology. Vol 17, No 1. Pp. 55-74.

Gregory, Henry. **NTU Psychotherapy: A Pluralist Approach.** Washington, D.C.: Progressive Life Center Publication.

[4]Myers, Linda (1988) **Understanding an Afrocentric World view: Introduction to an Optimal Psychology.** Dubuque, Iowa: Kendall/Hunt Publishing Co.

Azibo, DA **Liberation Psychology** (1992) Unpublished Manuscript presented at Temple University Department of African American Studies.

[5]Phillips, Frederick B. (1990) <u>NTU Psychotherapy: An Afrocentric Approach.</u> The Journal of Black Psychology. Vol 17, No 1. Pp. 55-74.

Harmonizing Families and Communities with Sacred Stones

[1]The diagram depicting the human family was created by Gerald 'Asaggai' Smith, an educational consultant and African-centered scholar in the Washington, D.C. community.

African Spirituality and Sacred Stones

[1]Diop, Cheikh Anta (1978) **The Cultural Unity of Black Africa.** Chicago: Third World Press.

[2]The primary sources for the parallel symbols within the various African spiritual systems are:

Edwards, Gary and Mason, John (1985) **Black Gods – Orisha Studies in the New World.** New York: Yoruba Theological Archministry

Lewis, Melchizedek (1993) **The Ancient Mysteries of Melchizedek: The New Revised Edition.** New York: MYL Publishers

Budge, Wallis E.A. (1969 reprint) **The Gods of the Egyptians (Vol 1&2)** New York: Dover Books.

Davidson, Gustav (1967) **A Dictionary of Angels, Including the Fallen Angels.** New York: The Free Press.

Amen, Ra Un Nefer (1990) **Mdu Neter** (Vol 1). New York: Khamit Corp.

Gonzalez-Wipplier, Migene (1981) **Santeria: African Magic in Latin America.** New York: Original Products.

Escape the Toxic Zone

[1]Byrd, Gary and John Harris (1995). **Escape From the Toxic Zone: A System of Survival Resource Guide.** New York: WLIB Radio 1190am. Escape the Toxic Zone is community service information packet prepared by WLIB for its listening audience.

[2]The primary sources for mineral properties, stones they are found in, as well as the functions in the body are:

Pookrum, Jewel, (1992) **Vitamins and Minerals From A to Z.** Michigan: J.E.W.E.L. Publications.

Jenson, Bernard (1983) **The Chemistry of Man.** California: Bernard Jenson International.

Arem, Joel (1973) **Rocks and Minerals.** Arizona: Geoscience Press, Inc.

[3]Walker, Morton. (1991) **The Power of Color.** New York: Avery Publishing

Vibrational Warfare

[1]**The Holy Bible. King James Version:** The Open Bible Edition. Tennessee: Royal Publishers. The quote may be found in Genesis, Ch 11.

[2]Hall, Manley. (1907) **Secret Teachings of All Ages.** California: Philosophical Research Society P.CLXXIV.

[3]Arguelles, Jose. (1987) **The Mayan Factor: Path Beyond Technology** New Mexico: Bear & Co.

[4]For in-depth science on the use of stone buildings as resonant broadcasting structures can be found in a series of books by Peter Thompkins:

Thompkins, Peter. (1971) **Secrets of the Great Pyramid.** New York: Harper & Row.

_____(1989) **Secrets of the Soil.** New York: Harper & Row.
_____(1973) **Secret Life of Plants.** New York: Harper & Row.

[5]Thompkins, Peter (1989) Secrets of the Soil. New York: Harper & Row. P.278-301. Thompkins clearly states "That the system of broadcasting cosmic energy with towers, obelisks, or pyramids goes back to the historical developers of structures, the Egyptians, stands to reason, but the proof of it is very recent..."

[6]Ibid, p280.

[7]Broad, William. "The Core of the Earth May Be A Gigantic Crystal of Iron" New York Times, April 4, 1995.

[8]Thompkins, Peter (1989) **Secrets of the Soil.** New York: Harper & Row. P.289-301.

[9]Pennick, Nigel. (1979) **The Ancient Science of Geomancy: Living in Harmony with the Earth.** California: CRCS Publications.

[10]Valerian, Valdamar. (1992 reprint) **The Matrix.** Washington: Leading Edge Research.

[11]Bell, Art (1996) HAARP: Weapon of Doom? Instrument of Peace. *After Dark with Art Bell*, a publication of CBC and TRN.

[12] Byrd, Gary and John Harris (1995). **Escape From the Toxic Zone: A System of Survival Resource Guide.** New York: WLIB Radio 1190am. Escape the Toxic Zone is community service information packet prepared by WLIB for its listening audience.

Bioresonance

[1]Monteith, Henry C. (1983) **Geometry and the Great Pyramid.** New Mexico: Sandia Laboratories.

[2]Walter, Nik *"The Geometry of Life: A Simple Pattern on Numbers Guides the Forms of Living Things"* The Washington Post, February 8, 1995.

[3]Baer, Randall and Vicki. (1987) **The Crystal Connection: A Guidebook for Personal and Planetary Ascension.** San Francisco: Harper & Row Pub.

[4]Cousins, Gabriel. (1986) **Spiritual Nutrition and the Rainbow Diet.** California: Cassandra Press.

[5]Byrd, Gary and John Harris (1995). **Escape From the Toxic Zone: A System of Survival Resource Guide.** New York: WLIB Radio 1190am. Escape the Toxic Zone is community service information packet prepared by WLIB for its listening audience.

[6]Raphaell, Katrina. (1985) **Crystal Enlightenment.** New Mexico: Aurora Press.

_____(1987) **Crystal Healing:** New Mexico: Aurora Press.

_____(1990) **Crystalline Transmission.** New Mexico: Aurora Press.

Katrina Raphaell's trilogy is an excellent resource for information on properties of the mineral kingdom.

[7]**Dorland's Illustrated Medical Dictionary.** 24th Ed. (1965) W.B. Saunders Co.,

[8]Adler, Vera, Stanley. (1970) **Finding of tile Third Eye.** Maine: Samuel Weiser, Inc.

For more information about the
Rocks of Ages, contact Ras Ben at:

Those Four Sounds
PO Box 25637
Philadelphia, PA 19144

www.Thosefoursounds.com